Architectural Design

Off the Radar

Guest-edited by Brian Carter
and Annette LeCuyer

 WILEY-ACADEMY

Architectural Design

Vol 73 No 1 Jan/Feb 2003

Editorial Offices
International House
Ealing Broadway Centre
London W5 5DB
T: +44 (0)20 8326 3800
F: +44 (0)20 8326 3801
E: architecturaldesign@wiley.co.uk

Editor
Helen Castle
Production
Mariangela Palazzi-Williams
Art Director
Christian Küsters ↘ CHK Design
Designer
Scott Bradley ↘ CHK Design
Picture Editor
Famida Rasheed

Advertisement Sales
01243 843272

Editorial Board
Denise Bratton, Adriaan Beukers,
André Chaszar, Peter Cook,
Max Fordham, Massimiliano
Fuksas, Edwin Heathcote, Anthony
Hunt, Charles Jencks, Jan Kaplicky,
Robert Maxwell, Jayne Merkel,
Monica Pidgeon, Antoine Predock,
Leon van Schaik

Contributing Editors
André Chaszar
Craig Kellogg
Jeremy Melvin
Jayne Merkel

ISBN 0-470-84571-6
Profile No 161

Abbreviated positions
t=top, b=bottom, c=centre, l=left, r=right
Cover image:
Jason Reed/Ryan McVay/Getty Images

Back cover image
The Svalbard Administration Building
© Jarmund / Vigsnaes AS Architects MNAL

_ΔD_ main section
pp 4, 5, 91 & 92 © Jarmund / Vigsnaes AS
Architects MNAL; p 7 © Richard Kroeker; p 8(t)
© Architect Gutmorgeth, photo: Gunther Wett; pp
8(b), 57, 58(t), 59, 61 & 63 © Daniel Malhão; p 9 ©
National Maritime Museum, London; pp 10 & 89 ©
Snohetta; pp 13, 17 & 55 © Studio Granda; pp 14 &
15 © Dennis Gilbert / VIEW; p 16 © Sigurgeir
Sigurjonsson; pp 18-20(t) photos: Rajesh Vora; p
20(b) photo: Rahul Mehrotra; pp 21-25 © Arup,
photos: Caroline Sohie and Roland Reinardy; pp
26-28(t&cl) © Heikkinen-Komonen Architects,
photos: Onerva Utriainen; p 28(cr) © Heikkinen-
Komonen Architects, photo: Mikko Heikkinen; pp
29-35 © German del Sol, Architect; pp 36-38 ©
Felipe Assadi, photos: Juan Purcell; p 39 © José
Cruz Ovalle, photo: Ana Turell; pp 40-42 © José
Cruz Ovalle, photos: Juan Purcell; pp 43-45 ©
Patrick Reynolds; pp 46, 54 & 56 © John Tuomey;
pp 48 & 50 © Dennis Gilbert / VIEW; pp 64, 65 & 67
© Paul Ott Photografiert; p 66 © Thomas
Jantscher; pp 68-69 © Serge Demailly; pp 70 &
72(t) photos: © Michael Awad; pp 71 & 74(c&bl)
photos: © James Dow; p 73 © Shim-Sutcliffe; p
74(cl) photo: Ed Burtynsky; pp 76-78 © Patkau
Architects Inc.; p 79 © Patkau / Croft Pelletier
Architectes Associés; pp 81-84(l) photos Michel
Legendre © Centre Canadien d' Architecture /
Canadian Centre for Architecture, Montreal; p
84(r) Photo Alain Laforest © Centre Canadien d'
Architecture / Canadian Centre for Architecture,
Montreal; p 85 photo: Jiri Havran; pp 87(t) & 88(b)
photos: Jan Olav Jensen; p 87(r) photo: Brian
Carter; p 93 courtesy Sverre Fehn; pp 95 & 97 ©
Annette LeCuyer; p 96(l) every effort has been
made to locate sources and credit material but
where this has not been possible our apologies are
extended; p 96(r) © Suzanne Ewing; p 100 © Tod
Williams Billie Tsien, photos: Russ Wooten

_ΔD+_ section
pp 102+(main)-105+ © Norman McGrath; p
102+(inset) courtesy of Tishman Realty &
Construction Co., Inc., photo: Norman McGrath; pp
106+ & 107+(r) © Buro Happold / Adam Wilson; p
107+(l) © Keegan Duigenan; pp 108-110+ ©
Edward Cullinan Architects; p 111+ © SHoP /
Sharples Holden Pasquarelli; p 112+(l) courtesy
Professor Dr. Ir. M van Tooren Faculty of Aerospace
Engineering, Delft University of Technology; p
112+(c) © Albacore Research Ltd; p 112+(r) ©
Kolatan / MacDonald Studio; p 113+ © Buro
Happold; p 114+ © Arup Acoustics; pp 116-117+
su11 Architecture+Design; pp118+, 122+(t) &
124+(b) © Paul Warchol / photography by Paul
Warchol; pp 119-121+ © James Carpenter Design
Associates, Inc.; p 122+(c) courtesy Toshiko Mori
Architect, photo: Nana Watanabe; pp 123+(l) &
124+(t) © Toshiko Mori Architect; p 123+(r) ©
Antoine Bootz; pp 126-127+ © Bob Sheil

Acknowledgments
We would like to thank the Taubman College of
Architecture and Urban Planning at the University
of Michigan for supporting the research for this
project. Completed during our sabbatical leaves
during the 2001–2002 academic year it was an
undertaking that was made possible only by that
generous gift of time. In addition, the essays by
Craig Dykers and by Tod Williams and Billie Tsien
that are included in this issue of _ΔD_ originated from
material initially developed with students there and
subsequently published in _Dimensions 15_ – the
annual journal of the college. The descriptions of
Shim Sutcliffe's Moorelands Camp and Muskoka
Boathouse were inspired by their 2000 Charles and
Ray Eames Lecture at the University of Michigan, a
lecture that was subsequently published in the
MAP series, and later informed by a series of
meetings and conversations with the architects.
We would also like to thank Rebecca Price,
architecture librarian at the University of Michigan,
for her invaluable help and advice.

We are especially grateful to Helen Castle for
her enthusiasm, patience and continued
encouragement. She was responsive to the idea of
an issue of _ΔD_ dedicated to an exploration of
architecture at the edge and nurtured it over time.
In addition Famida Rasheed, Mariangela Palazzi
Williams, Abigail Grater and Caroline Ellerby at the
John Wiley office and the graphic designer
Christian Küsters all worked extremely hard to
prepare the material for publication and make it
coherent, legible and thoughtfully set out on the
printed page.

This issue of _ΔD_ has been realised with the
assistance and cooperation of many architects,
photographers and colleagues around the world.
Without their inspiration and persistent enthusiasm
to make architecture in circumstances that were
frequently adverse there would be no reason for this
issue. In addition, without their generosity and
willingness to meet, talk and arrange for us to visit
their work, this publication and the consideration of
the edge that it has prompted would not have been so
rewarding or challenging. BC/AWL

Published in Great Britain in 2003 by Wiley-
Academy, a division of John Wiley & Sons Ltd
Copyright © 2003, John Wiley & Sons Ltd, The
Atrium, Southern Gate, Chichester, West Sussex
PO19 8SQ, England, Telephone (+44) 1243 779777
Email (for orders and customer service enquiries):
cs-books@wiley.co.uk Visit our Home Page on
www.wileyeurope.com or www.wiley.com

Subscription Offices UK
John Wiley & Sons Ltd.
Journals Administration Department
1 Oldlands Way, Bognor Regis
West Sussex, PO22 9SA
T: +44 (0)1243 843272
F: +44 (0)1243 843232
E: cs-journals@wiley.co.uk

Annual Subscription Rates 2003
Institutional Rate: UK £160
Personal Rate: UK £99
Student Rate: UK £70
Institutional Rate: US $240
Personal Rate: US $150
Student Rate: US $105
_ΔD_ is published bi-monthly.
Prices are for six issues and include
postage and handling charges.
Periodicals postage paid at Jamaica,
NY 11431. Air freight and mailing in the
USA by Publications Expediting Services
Inc, 200 Meacham Avenue, Elmont,
NY 11003

Single Issues UK: £22.50
Single Issues outside UK: US $45.00
Details of postage and packing charges
available on request

Postmaster
Send address changes to _ΔD_ Publications
Expediting Services, 200 Meacham Avenue,
Elmont, NY 11003

Printed in Italy. All prices are subject
to change without notice.
[ISSN: 0003-8504]

Off the Radar

Guest-edited by Brian Carter
and Annette LeCuyer

As is sometimes the case when travelling, neither the route nor the final destination is anticipated at the outset. Brian Carter and Annette LeCuyer first suggested an idea for an issue of ⌂ to me when they were planning to travel for a year. What has emerged, through a persistent search and considered process of selection and editing on their part, is a collection of exceptional evenness and quality. It poses the question of what it takes to be working successfully at the geographical, economic or political periphery. What transpires is an acute awareness of one's own intentions and ambitions. This has to be combined with a pragmatic resourcefulness that is noted by John Patkau when he describes how, working in Canada's Pacific Northwest, it is difficult to call upon the specialist advice or skills that are taken for granted by many US and UK practices. An affinity to climate, site and local communities also often requires materials and construction to be treated with an exceptional integrity. A rootedness and connection to locality appear to attract architects who desire not only to be answerable to local societies but also to invest in craft and the physical quality of the artifact over global market constraints on time and standardisation. What also sets many of these architects apart is a staunch ability to pursue their vision and beliefs. Perhaps this is most apparent in German del Sol's description of his work where he speaks about his resolve to practise in his own native country of Chile, harnessing what might be regarded as its frustrating attributes of remoteness and slowness and using them to the benefit of architecture. For what has to be remembered is that throughout history – whether in the 15th-century Vicenza of Palladio or in the early 20th-century Finland of Alvar Aalto – the edge has been essential and fecund ground for architecture. ⌂

'Contrary to popular belief, the outskirts are not where the world ends — they are precisely the place where it begins to unfurl.'—Joseph Brodsky [1]

In developing the theme for this issue, our initial thoughts focused on geography – on searching out architecture in places that are physically remote and beyond popular centres of architectural debate. These debates are frequently centred around predictable axes that connect New York, Los Angeles and London, or Rotterdam, Basel and Genoa. But while these lines around which bodies of thought and investigation tend to rotate may be imaginary, they are all too often endorsed and made exclusive by the media, professional journals and advertising.

However, forces at the periphery have been combining in ways that tend to redraw maps and suggest other worlds. The redefinition of political boundaries, formulation of trade agreements and impact of a series of cataclysmic international events have created new countries, territories and concerns that are impinging both directly and indirectly on modern architecture. At the same time cheap airlines have located new destinations with low landing fees and little-known hinterlands; there has been an increasing interest in travelling off the beaten track; Wallpaper* has championed an international interest in design that extends beyond the narrow boundaries of the profession; and even within the profession the oscillation between centre and edge has been reflected in the recent history of the Pritzker Prize, with awards to Foster, Piano, Gehry, Koolhaas and Herzog & de Meuron interspersed with recognition of Sverre Fehn and Glenn Murcutt.

The focus on geography proved rewarding and has helped to tease out work that is located in extreme northern and southern latitudes with buildings not only in Europe, but in Africa, Asia, New Zealand and the Americas. However, it also became clear that it is increasingly difficult to be 'off the radar'. Not only do efficient and economic intercontinental transportation systems make the world more accessible, but improved electronic communication offers virtually instant connections to even the most remote places. Combined these developments create an intricate web of mutual awareness that extends around the globe. Nevertheless, because the production of architecture is a physical as well as conceptual act, geography does remain a significant constraint. As this selected work demonstrates, in these distinct settings, factors such as terrain, climate, materials and available construction technologies remain important considerations in the making of architecture.

Under closer inspection, the interest in architects working 'off the radar' became more complex, and the concept of distance was enriched when it was understood not only in physical but also in political and economic terms. Some of the places initially identified as being geographically remote are coincidentally also in the throes of political, economic and social change. Architects in these places consequently find themselves at another kind of edge, a threshold to a future that is being shaped by markedly different factors than in the recent past. These circumstances have a direct bearing not only on the nature of patronage but also on construction culture. In Norway, for example, the revenues from North Sea oil have dramatically increased the potential for public and private patronage, while in Portugal and Ireland the injection of capital arising from their entry into the European Community is fundamentally changing traditional building cultures towards more industrialised, international modes of production. However, the momentum is not always forward in the direction of increasingly democratic societies and improving economies. A recent article in the Financial Times, for example, observes that Argentina – a nation that has long been concerned by its position 'at the edge of the world' – was during the 1990s 'the most frequently cited example of the power of globalisation to bring nations together. [Argentina is now] moving in the opposite direction, falling into isolation despite its best efforts. It is a stunning example of globalisation in reverse'.[2]

This more complex understanding of distance in turn led to the concept of 'off the radar' being developed further through the consideration of architecture commissioned for groups that have been marginalised politically, socially and economically. The initiatives of the Indigo Foundation and the Drukpa Kargyud Trust, as well as those of governments across Scandinavia, have given architects a central role in the design of improved educational systems in places close to the equator, in the Himalayas and beyond the Arctic Circle. This work, designed by architects who are outside of yet working for indigenous communities, may at first sight appear to have paternalistic or colonial overtones. However, in these particular projects architecture is being used not to register imperial authority but instead as a means of supporting local communities and building economies, enhancing the education, skills and capacities of local people, and conserving both cultural and natural landscapes.

While marginalisation is often imposed from without, it may also grow voluntarily from within. French Canadians, having long perceived themselves as culturally threatened, instigated a self-imposed agenda of political and economic isolation. A series of referendums, which posed the question of Quebec's independence from Canada, were only narrowly defeated and the separatist question remains a persistent issue in Canada. Not surprisingly, architecture in Quebec has been seen as an instrument of reinforcing and developing French cultural identity. In this context, the recent exhibition of the work of young Montreal architects initiated by the Canadian Centre for Architecture was surprisingly doubled-edged. Instead of being introverted, it was decidedly outward looking and engaged, reacting to the significant events of 11 September 2001 – a new horizon that has been drawn at the edge of previous understanding and experience.

With the understanding that distance can be psychological as well as physical, 'off the radar' considers architects who, instead of conforming with the expectations of contemporary building practice, are pushing at the edge with their focused explorations of unconventional or forgotten materials. Tod Williams and Billie Tsien, whose work is centred in Manhattan, are certainly not geographically or culturally isolated. However, by consciously distancing themselves from fast-track production and seeking ways to incorporate craft in design and construction, they are exploring new territory. That they have been able to apply this strategy to the design and fabrication of the facade of the Museum of American Folk Art, a major public building in New York, is a notable achievement.

Likewise, the work of the French architect Gilles Perraudin in the heart of Europe abandons the thin-layered construction that has become a contemporary norm in favour of thick, heavy load-bearing masonry construction for buildings in the south of France. Although Perraudin lives and works in the shadow of the Pont du Gard, this work is not nostalgic for the past but instead is a response to the environmental concerns that have – to varying degrees in different countries – become increasingly important factors in shaping architecture.

The concerted investigations of wood in buildings have proved fertile ground for architects in many parts of the world. A tiny meeting house, designed by Richard Kroeker for a First Nation band at Eskasoni in Nova Scotia, explores the potential of green timber, while the architect Jose Cruz Ovalle has used wood to construct large industrial spaces for his clients in Chile. These explorations, almost invariably carried out with the close collaboration of enlightened industries, materials scientists and structural engineers, demonstrate the value of multidisciplinary approaches to design – a process that almost invariably ventures into new territory and advances the boundaries of knowledge about materials, systems and building performance.

Many of these projects underline the importance of inspired patronage, an aspect of architecture all too often overlooked yet clearly vital to the development of innovative architectural research and critical practice. In small communities or remote settings, both clients and architects may have little alternative but to be more resourceful and open-minded about their roles and their work. So in Iceland and Portugal, moves by municipal and regional authorities to involve architects in infrastructure design have been rewarding, while in Chile the architect German del Sol has taken on the role of developer to realise hotel projects that at the time were based on unproven business models.

Changing patterns of living and working are also sponsoring the development of new and hybrid programmes. Confronted with this alternative territory, architects are being challenged to rethink the design of the house, the form of public buildings and the extent of the civic realm – issues that are focused through the lenses of different cultures in projects as diverse as a village house in India and a

Page 5
The Svalbard Administration Building, designed by Jarmund/Vigsnaes, provides a civic outpost for a settlement north of the Arctic Circle.

Right
A project in Nova Scotia designed by Richard Kroeker with students at Dalhousie University, Faculty of Architecture, uses small-section green timber to create a meeting house for a local First Nation community.

collection depot for Internet shoppers in Santiago. In the Netherlands and Norway, ingenuity is evident in the development of hospitals that include hotels for short-stay patients and visitors, together with community centres and educational facilities for children. These projects, although partially driven by economic arguments linked to the relative costs of hotel and hospital bedspaces, are also aimed at improving health care by helping patients recuperate in more congenial surroundings and with the support of family, friends and community. So the Sykehotellet at the Nytt Rikshospital in Oslo, designed by Div.A Architects, and Mecanoo's scheme for the Gezondheidspark in Dordrecht both move away from previously understood institutional models and the equally predictable architecture that resulted, to the design of new building types in cities.

Above
The sweeping roof designed for a supermarket for Mpreis in the Tyrol, provides sheltered parking in the winter and a covered market for the village during the summer months.

Right
A house hidden within the shell of houses in the village of Alenquer in Portugal.

Notes
1. Joseph Brodsky, 'On Derek Walcott', *New York Review of Books*, 10 November 1983, p 39.
2. Thomas Catan, 'Crisis sweeps Argentina back towards the edge of the world', *Financial Times*, 22–23 June 2002, p 26.

Hybrids are also detectable in the countryside. In Austria a series of small new fire stations have been designed to incorporate multi-use halls for the community. These small projects have not only provided the basis for architectural competitions organised by the state and a testing ground for young architectural practices, but have also created a number of fine new civic buildings in village centres. Another innovative programme, also in Austria, was initiated by a private developer. When Mpreis – a supermarket chain with shops in the Tyrol – decided to build a new outlet in the village of Leutasch, architect Erich Gutmorgeth proposed a scheme with a vast, light oversailing roof to cover not only the supermarket but also its car parking, an adjacent bank and a post office. This roof creates a civic space that is used for for weekly markets during the summer and provides snow-free parking in winter.

Like distance, time is a critical factor in reinforcing a sense of connection or isolation. In contrast with buildings, which have traditionally been designed to be timeless, we now live in a world of aggressively market-based economies where that sense of time has been compressed and information travels instantaneously to points near and far. Reflecting these cultural priorities, the anticipated life of buildings suddenly seems to have reduced. At the same time the media's increased interest in architecture has tended to transform design and construction into a fast-moving digitally driven process that produces fashionable artefacts that can be consumed quickly and promise instant gratification. But consideration of work 'off the radar' offers alternatives.

In the Irish village of Letterfrack, work has been under way for more than 10 years and promises to continue for perhaps as long again under the thoughtful direction of architects Sheila O'Donnell and John Tuomey as well as the community. In this work – as in that of Ernst Giselbrecht at Seggau, Aires Mateus at Alenquer, and Jarmund/Vigsnaes in Svalbard – time in architecture also embraces the consideration of how contemporary interventions, often hidden, might revitalise both ruins and existing inhabited buildings to project a new kind of life into a place.

Architects are frequently dismissed as aesthetes who are out of touch with the social, political and economic context within which they design and build. In contrast, this work is evidence of architects who have actively sought out engagement and who are forging alternatives to the frequently perceived marginalisation of the profession. This issue of ◬ probes at the periphery to examine the work of architects at the threshold of political and economic change, and in settings that are both physically and mentally distant from the 'centre'. This is an ever-changing periphery, an illusory horizon where critical axes can be extended and inspiration found through diverse and informed considerations of design. ◬ BC AWL

Edgelessness

Sixteenth-century Portuguese adventurer Ferdinand Magellan is famous for having led the first voyage to circumnavigate the globe. Here **Craig Dykers**, a principal of Snøhetta architects in Norway, retells the story of Magellan as an allegory, which sheds light on the need for a new 'edgeless sensitivity to place' able to transcend the limitations of time and space as well as the physical world of built objects.

HERNANDO DE MAGALLANES.
Cavallero Portugues, descubridor del
Estrecho de su nombre.

On Saturday, 7 September 1522 the weather-beaten galleon *Victoria* arrived in Spain. It was the only remaining vessel of those that had set out on Ferdinand Magellan's epic 62,880-kilometre voyage, and it had completed the first circumnavigation of the globe in human history. Magellan had died en route in less than heroic circumstances, and on the return of the expedition his biographer delivered his valuable diary to awaiting Spanish officials. Magellan had initiated that record four years earlier on Tuesday, 20 September 1519, the day the ship had left port.

With some surprise the Spaniards noted that in the diary the day the ship returned was in fact claimed to be 6 September. The dates were checked with the ship's log, and it was found that no mistake had been made, no days had been left out. The Spaniards did not understand how the ship's crew could have forgotten a full day in the log, and it was certain that all of Spain could not have inadvertently added a day to their calendars. Debate continued for decades to explain why the arrival date in the ship's log was one day behind the same calendar date in Spain.

This first circumnavigation of the earth had exposed one of the fundamental effects of living on a spinning, spherical, solar-centric planet; the ship had unknowingly crossed the date line, and a solar day had been lost in the expedition's westward travels.

It had been reasonably well established at the time that the world was round, and with Magellan's venture its geometry had been proven. Yet the spherical nature of the earth was not entirely appreciated; the loss of a day as a consequence of westerly travel around the world could not be explained. Although the event occurred nearly 500 years ago, the concept of the date line is still difficult to grasp today.

However, other insights beyond the formal encirclement of the globe can be gained from

Magellan's voyage. His remaining ship, *Victoria*, returned to Europe without him, and here there are clues that relate this story to limitations of society as well as those of geometry. Magellan was both an intelligent politician and a well-travelled captain. Born to Portuguese nobility, his expedition began in the courts of Portugal where he tried to convince the sovereign Dom Manuel I to fund his navigation of a passage around the planet. This voyage was fuelled by Magellan's previous excursions to the Orient, discussions with Pacific mariners and his knowledge of the exploits of explorers such as Marco Polo. But while the Portuguese court was intrigued, he could not stir up enough enthusiasm to secure the resources necessary to complete the expedition. As a consequence, Magellan turned his attention to rival Spain, his only other viable source of patronage yet one that he anticipated having similar difficulties in securing.

At the time the Spanish were eager to find some means of breaking the Portuguese monopoly of the then lucrative natural resources of the Spice Islands and Moluccas in the Indian Ocean. After a long series of wars and the surprising appearance of the New World where India was supposed to be, Portuguese ownership of the Spice Islands was granted by a papal decree. In a moment of unbelievable wit Pope Alexander VI, according to popular accounts, placed a flat map of the world upon the table, drew a line across the map from top to bottom through the Atlantic and parts of the Americas, and claimed that all non-Christian lands to the east of the demarcation would belong to Portugal and all lands to the west to Spain. Hence the Portuguese language is found in Brazil where the line crossed through its outermost point, and Spanish is found in the remainder of Latin America. The so-called Indies were divided into East and West, and the Spice Islands, being to the east of this line on the map, fell into the hands of the Portuguese.

Sailing south along the coast of Africa and then east across the Indian Ocean, the Portuguese navigated freely within their realm to reach the East Indies. Magellan convinced the Spanish and Carlos I that he could sail to the west across the papal demarcation in the Atlantic, around South America and – by reason of the world being round without the limitations of edges found on the flat projection used by the pope – he would eventually land at the Spice Islands across the Pacific Ocean. This would place the islands to the west of the papal divide and allow the Spanish to claim the lands for themselves. The Spanish decided to support Magellan's venture.

By the standards of the day, Magellan was considered a thoughtful captain. At the start of the voyage he was seen as somewhat benign and resourceful, and garnered considerable respect from his crew. He loaded sufficient types of food to allay scurvy and his crew was healthy. The first portion of the journey was strenuous and the fleet laboured to round the southern point of South America. Reaching the enormous basin at the mouth of the Rio de la Plata, they thought they had reached the end of the continent. However, after a considerable period, realising their error they again headed southward where they passed through straits north of Cape Horn – now given Magellan's name – and thanks to good weather somewhat unceremoniously entered the Pacific Ocean becoming the first Europeans to sail this route from the east.

This was followed by an arduous crossing of the planet's largest body of water, the limits of which were at the time unknown to the weary fleet. While there were educated estimates of the size of the ocean, Magellan and his crew would have likely remained restless during the long passage across the island-free southeast Pacific.

On reaching the first Pacific islands and encountering native islanders, the expedition promptly adopted the European evangelical posture of converting indigenous peoples to Christianity and claiming lands for the court. And the added assurance that their journey into the Pacific was the first from the east provided the captain and crew with the self-confidence of being messengers of God and Crown.

At this stage, Magellan allowed the first groups of islanders he encountered to maintain their indigenous religions together with Christianity, provided they somehow muttered allegiance to a European sovereign and God. However, in time and as greater distances were covered, Magellan's self-confidence grew, turning to arrogance. By the time he reached the Philippines he no longer allowed for leniency when civilising native peoples. At the island province of Cebu in the Philippines he forced a village of nearly 2000 natives to give up their deeply rooted religious beliefs and alliances. Being of greater numbers, the islanders strongly resisted. But after a series of protracted and complicated formal engagements with various leaders of the native community, Magellan assured his crew that the village could be subjugated to Spanish will with the evangelical intervention of God and the Holy Virgin.

Leaving his mariners behind, he led three small boats with a few untrained and lightly armed guards.

Page 9
Engraving of the Portuguese navigator Ferdinand Magellan (c 1480–1521).

Opposite
The New Library of Alexandria in Egypt, opened in the spring of 2002, was designed by the Norwegian group of architects Snøhetta as a revival of the ancient library in the city founded by Alexander the Great. Adopting a vast circular form alongside the circular harbour at Alexandria, it is intended to symbolise the cyclical nature of knowledge. Rejuvenating the city's ancient reputation for scholarship, its aim is to revitalise Alexandria and the region as a centre of culture and learning. The geography of the economic and cultural centres of the world are never still. This was emphasised and accelerated by the opening of the New World after the explorations of Magellan, but has continued ever since at a rapid pace with the onset of industrialisation and globalism.

As they beached at Mactan, weighed down by ungainly military garb, the enraged natives mutilated Magellan's body so badly that the remaining crew could not retrieve even the most basic scrap of clothing or identification of their captain who had shown to them the true physical nature of the planet on which they lived.

But the final twist of this story has yet to unfold. Prior to this voyage, Magellan had been to the Moluccas on other expeditions financed from Portugal. He was familiar with the area and on one occasion had purchased a young Malayan slave sent to auction from Limasawa, one of the islands at the rim of Sumatra. This young slave returned to Europe with him and was trained as his manservant. By his adolescence, the boy had been educated in European matters and languages, and had probably forgotten much of his past and the island of his origin, having been removed at a very young age. This trusted companion and manservant, now known only as Enrique, was to accompany Magellan on his expedition around the world.

After crossing the Pacific and returning to previously known Spanish and Portuguese territory in Asia, the fleet landed on the Visayan Archipelago in the Philippines. On disembarking the crew met with the indigenous islanders. They had difficulty communicating as the crew were not familiar with the language of the islanders. But soon Magellan and his crew heard laughter from another crowd nearby. At the centre of this crowd stood Enrique who had returned to his homeland and after decades of separation recalled the language of his birthplace.

The unique consequence of this event was that Enrique, the manservant, was in fact the first person to circumnavigate the earth, albeit over a period of some 20 years between embarkation and return. At this moment Magellan would have definitively realised that his assumptions regarding the globe were correct, having taken Enrique home by travelling westward. Yet he did not, as we do not today, credit the remarkable feat of the first circumnavigation of the world to a virtually nameless servant.

The world is not necessarily what we make of it. It is both the stories we tell about it and the story it wants to tell us. While objects at the Euclidean level appear uncomplicated and therefore become useful symbols for larger ideas, they do not exist solely as forms without relation to the places they inhabit. Consequence and form are inseparable in time.

During the past 30 years astronomers have mapped the locations of over a million galaxies distributed in three dimensions throughout observable space. The resulting, almost incomprehensible map shows the largest-scale structure ever seen by the human eye and represents clusters of galaxies in a volume of over 200 million light years in all directions – a beautifully lacy, membranous pattern, a unique geometry that incorporates our planet and galaxy.

This new view of the world, similar to the first photographs of the earth taken by astronauts, separates now from the past. Knowledge of our world has shifted from primitive sketches of a limited, earth-centred planet to globes spinning around the sun. Understanding has now shifted yet again to a fluid space-and-time continuum. Time and space no longer exist as discrete entities. Our universe appears to be filled with a sparkling water-like fluid of curving, light-emitting, absorbing and reflecting currents meandering through numerous tides of dimension. Like the waters of the Pacific under Magellan's pioneering ships, this vast galactic ocean has unknown shores across unimaginable distances. But it will not be the discovery of distant shores that lends appreciation of our place on this map. As with the Magellan voyage, the circumnavigation of this place will prove more complex than simply illustrating its physical layout.

Closed geometrical forms artificially separate time and space, but this useful limitation is far from essential. It would be considered ridiculous to physically separate the events of one day, one season or one year from the next, despite their clear divisions on a calendar. While there may be a middle of the day, there is neither an edge nor a centre to time. The things we create on, over and within our world are ultimately manifestations of a subtle and intricate intrigue. Objects, as they are created, embody both intuitive and formal human sensibilities. As architects we still have the ability to entertain less limited, edgeless sensitivities of our place. And as this occurs, creativity will evolve and architecture as we know it will become a backwash in the memories of our descendants. ◬

Craig Dykers is a founding partner of Snøhetta. Since moving to Norway in 1989 he has been involved in the design of major projects in Europe, the Middle East and the US. He was co-designer for the New Library of Alexandria in Egypt, designer for the Norwegian Embassy in Berlin and is currently co-designer for the new National Opera in Norway. He is a member of the Norwegian Architecture Association (NAL) and has served as diploma adjudicator at the Architectural College in Oslo. He has lectured in Europe, Asia and the US.

Located at the Arctic Circle, Iceland, a small island set in the broad expanse of the Atlantic Ocean, is disconnected from Europe and America. Created at the meeting of the shifting tectonic plates of the earth's crust, it is a primal place of active volcanoes, geysers and geothermal springs. Nothing is stable — it is land eroded by adverse weather and constantly reshaped by earthquakes, volcanic action and glaciers. Lava fields are extensive and only one per cent of the land surface is tilled soil. Trees are rare. With a population of 275,000, settlements are small, widely scattered and dominated by the vast scale and strange characteristics of the land, the coastline and the ocean. The weather is dramatic. It changes rapidly, footprints are quickly erased and for several months of the year daylight is limited. Inhabiting these extremes demands a tuning of the senses, persistence and an acute awareness of the nature of the landscape.

Studio Granda

Since opening its office in 1987, Studio Granda has founded a base for critical practice in Iceland that is noticeably shaped by the relationships between architecture and landscape. Their competition-winning scheme for the City Hall in Reykjavik and subsequent commissions to design the Supreme Court of Iceland and the National Gallery there, have successfully defined significant new civic places and a clear commitment to modern architecture in the capital city of this remote island. These civic projects have been inspired and strongly influenced by the expansiveness and rugged beauty of the ever-present natural surroundings.

Living and working in this relatively isolated country – a parliamentary democracy founded in 1944 where the majority of the population lives in Reykjavik and the architectural community totals 305 people – Studio Granda has had both the incentive and the opportunity to explore a wide field of design. These explorations have directed the practice to the design of furniture, interiors and lighting and an increasing involvement in the planning of urban infrastructure. Commissioned to develop designs for bridges, highway interchanges, and car-parking structures, Studio Granda has been working alongside civil engineers, urban planners, landscape architects and artists on projects that have required the architects to carefully consider relationships between architecture and design within the expansive settings of Iceland's extraordinary landscapes.

Kringlan Shopping Centre

A new car park has been planned to serve the Kringlan Shopping Centre, situated close to a residential area close to the centre of Reykjavik. Here, Studio Granda organised a design team that included not only structural and service engineers but also landscape architects and the Icelandic artist Kristinn E Hrafnsson. This collaborative approach resulted in the

radical transformation of what is otherwise an invariably banal building type.

In an attempt to mediate between the city and nature and between big-box retail, expansive roads and nearby housing, the new car park was considered as a constructed landscape, not a building. Planned on two levels the parking decks are pushed into the ground at an angle against the natural fall of the site. This enabled a realigned service ramp on the eastern side to be used for access as well as a connection between the two parking levels. It also supplements a new connecting ramp constructed between the two parking levels at the south end of the structure. The alignment of the parking decks juxtaposes the constructed and natural landscapes in a way that redefines the horizon. Views from the upper parking deck are being directed out beyond the skyline of the city to distant mountains. Framed by lines of extended columns that form tall steel light-posts across the upper deck, these long views focus attention on the rugged topography, the expanse of the sky and the inevitable drama of the rapidly changing weather that swirls around the island.

Viewed in its immediate setting, this scheme is also obviously more than a place for parking cars. A pedestrian promenade formed along the entire western edge of the car park defines a new garden at the entrance to the shopping mall and connects to a public square that has been created at the northeastern end of the parking structure. Here, the collaborative efforts of architect, artist, landscape architect and engineer are clearly legible. Paved with local basalt and defined by a wall of steel sheet piling, this square contains a small tower with a pedestrian bridge that connects to the upper parking deck. The tower, built of coursed ashlar basalt, reads as a rugged fragment. It contains the stair between the two parking levels but is also a contemporary treasure house with a sealed room where lead caskets containing objects selected from the shopping mall on opening day are stored. Access is through a large rusted steel door, and the significance of the room inside is signalled by a monumental lintel inscribed with the word '*Geymsla*' – store. This inscription also forms part of a longer poem. Combined with specially made lettered waste-bins and steel drain-cover plates, it introduces an inscription across the newly constructed landscape and makes the square an unlikely yet compelling civic space at this gateway of consumption.

The perimeter of the car park is defined by a retaining wall again constructed of steel sheet piling. Along its eastern edge, it has been shaped to follow the curve of the road, and as a result a tapering crevasse within the parking decks becomes another new element in the landscape. It is filled with trees

and irrigated with surface water from large steel gargoyles at the upper deck that freeze dramatically in winter. This crevasse also incorporates a sweeping pedestrian stairway of steel that transforms the connection between the two parking levels with an almost theatrical flourish. The trees – rare in the Icelandic landscape – introduce dappled light and greenery into the otherwise harsh environment of car parking and become natural analogues to be read alongside the tall, steel light-columns.

Studio Granda has considered not only the tectonic qualities but also the poetic readings of materials in the design of their projects. The palette of materials selected for the car park recalls the earth in ways that help emphasise the connections between building and landscape. The local basalt is cut meticulously and the concrete slabs have been cast with the smoothness of marble and held away from the sheet-metal piling of the perimeter wall. This detail brings natural light into the lower parking level while highlighting the flushness of the soffit and the changing colours of the corrugated face of the steel that so vividly record the weather over time. These choices work well in a place where natural light is clear yet ever changing and the primal colours, textures and shapes of the ground predominate.

Its projects have been planned to satisfy the pragmatic needs of pedestrian access, traffic flow and mass shopping that are increasingly familiar throughout the world. However, Studio Granda has successfully transformed these banal elements of modern life into works of art that are firmly rooted in the very different settings of the extraordinary Icelandic landscape.

Kringlan Shopping Centre, Reykjavik, 1999

Opposite
The stone store and pedestrian staircase on the edge of a new entrance square.

Above
The car-parking structure defines a new landscaped garden alongside the existing shopping centre.

The Kringlumyrarbraut Bridge

The Kringlumyrarbraut Bridge was designed to enable pedestrians to cross a six-lane road and connect two important recreational areas on the outskirts of Reykjavik. Situated in a low valley and beside a small fjord, the areas are sheltered places that catch the sun and as a result are popular destinations for walkers. However, the impact of the highway, which cuts across the fjord and separates the sea from the sheltered valley, is significant. Consequently, the new footbridge was designed as an attempt to reconstruct the ground.

By realigning an existing footpath, the approach to the bridge has been threaded between an exit from the highway and a mature woodland. This adjustment of the siting, together with the development of the design to ramp the bridge deck, generated a dynamic changing section for the structure. The form is accentuated by the extension of the handrail along the northern side of the bridge to create a screen that helps to cut out both the distraction and noise of the fast-flowing traffic below and the chilling north wind. The sweeping handrail also directs the views of pedestrians on the bridge out towards the ocean, and the bridge becomes a flying footpath enabling walkers to cross the transformed landscape, while for drivers its hazy lightness recalls the mists that commonly drift across the valley.

**Kringlumyrarbraut Bridge,
Reykjavik, 1995**

Above
A light screen on the northern side of the footbridge helps to mitigate noise and wind while focusing the view towards the ocean.

Right, top
The new pedestrian footbridge curves to connect two popular recreational areas on the outskirts of Reykjavik.

Right, bottom
Footbridge sections.

Highway Interchange at Höfdabakkabru

By contrast, the principal challenge in designing a highway interchange at Höfdabakkabru, which bridges a four-lane main road and connects with a secondary road into Reykjavik, was to integrate a large-scale object into the immediate setting and to engage the landscape of the horizon. This task was made more complex by different perceptions of the interchange – from those of passengers in fast- and slow-moving vehicles to stationary cars, pedestrians and people in surrounding buildings.

As a result, the huge concrete flank walls have been shaped and are asymmetrical so as to integrate them into the sloping site. Other walls, finished with hard, shiny black synthetic flint, form a backdrop against which it is possible to read the changing streams of colour created by the fast-moving vehicles on the highway. Columns supporting the bridge and dividing the lanes of traffic have been shaped in steel and painted bright colours in order to create a distinctive line of measure along the road that can be read by drivers moving at speed. In contrast, the choice of materials and detailing where pedestrians use the bridge as a crossing reflects the scale of the human body and its slower pace of movement. Here, an emphatic handrail, cut from hardwood that is relatively warm to the touch and shaped to the size and proportions of a tree trunk, gives the bridge a legibility from the road and offers a sense of security for pedestrians in an environment otherwise dominated by the machine. Ð BC

Above
**Höfdabakkabru Bridge,
Reykjavik, 1995**

'It is important to recognise that architecture is no longer the spectacle of the city in South Asia... In the urban context of South Asia there exists a physical duality of what I call the static city and the kinetic city. The static city is represented through architecture and is monumental, static and built in permanent materials. Its high point was after the sixties when corporate architecture arose in the commercial districts of Bombay. Similarly, during colonial times, the restructuring of the historic fort area signaled a change in the direction of the city. The British represented their power through the great neo-Gothic buildings.

These were moments where architecture was the spectacle of the city. In the kinetic city, which is the city of motion, the *kuttcha* city built of temporary materials, processions and festivals forms the spectacle and memory of the city. So the issues architects have to grapple with go beyond what is conventionally the role of the architect. We have to read these varied realities and this becomes the generator of practice, its inspirations and nourishment.'[1]

Two recent projects in India – the House at Khim by Rahul Mehrotra and the Druk White School at Ladakh by Arup/Arup Associates – highlight the varied realities there and illustrate how they have generated different approaches to design and practice.

Rahul Mehrotra

In designing a modest house for a young film maker and his family, the architect Rahul Mehrotra was confronted with both the potential and the contradictions highlighted in his description of the static and the kinetic city. Built on a one-acre site in the Alibag district of the village of Khim, situated across the harbour from Bombay, the house provides a weekend retreat for the family away from their busy day-to-day life in the city. As a result, the design has to address the differing lifestyles of the client – a relatively affluent urban family – and the rural villagers who are their neighbours.

Mehrotra has spoken of how 'in the way that you can make the kinetic and the static city work together you can make the poor and rich live together'.[2] In the plan that he has devised for

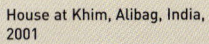
House at Khim, Alibag, India, 2001

Above
The house viewed from the forest with the curved roof sheltering a verandah.

Right
Metal roof viewed through wall.

Opposite
The built landscape of Ladakh.

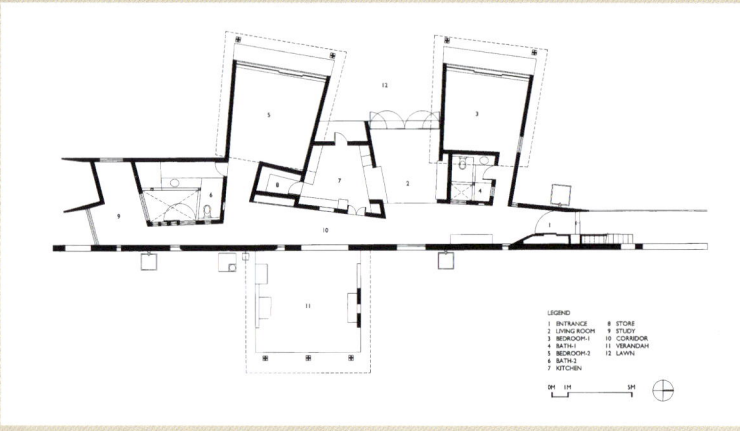

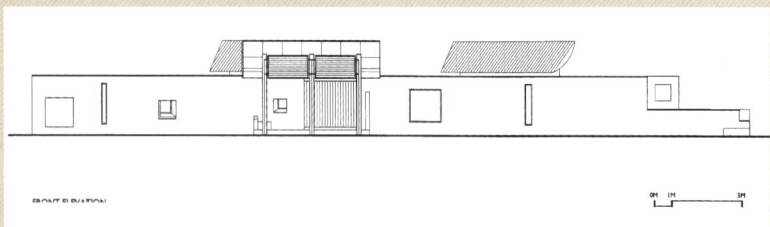

this particular project, the house divides the site into two conspicuously different spaces. Defined by a wall, the one to the east is an L-shaped forested landscape that is shaded by teak trees. Connected to the existing village, it forms a new shared public space.

The new boundary wall is built of stone. The use of this local material, which is exposed on the eastern face, helps to integrate the wall with the site but at the same time defines a new and obvious constructed element within this predominantly natural landscape. One of the main living spaces of the house has been planned on this side of the wall. Designed as a verandah, it opens out to the wooded site and the village beyond. The space is defined by low walls and shaded by a curved metal roof. Supported on slender steel columns and clad with industrial metal decking, the lightness and materiality of the roof are in sharp contrast with the heavy local-stone wall. It is a space that also recalls the informal shelters constructed between the walled compounds of local villages, and has been planned so that it can be used by both the owners of the house and the residents of Khim.

The same stone wall also encloses space on the opposite side that has been created specifically for use by the owners. These more private rooms of the house are placed on the western side of the wall with access from a long single-loaded corridor defined by the wall. A series of other spaces – a second living room, kitchen and a study together with two bedrooms and bathrooms – have been planned around new gardens. Here too the wall is finished differently, with sections that have been rendered with a pebble concrete finish and also painted to create abstract patterns and episodic moments that are visible only within the private realm of the house.

In describing new houses in Delhi and Bombay that have been designed like Palladian villas, Mehrotra refers to the way that 'architecture can polarise a society'.[3] However, he has also noted that 'you can design a house that doesn't establish that sense of discomfort. Architecture plays a role and in our societies, which are highly polarised and within which exist incredible disparities, any step towards dissolving some of that is important'.[4]

This scheme successfully develops a large open site at the edge of a village to create not only a private house but also new public places that can be shared by owners and local villagers alike. In forming these different spaces and juxtaposing the opposing vocabularies of static and kinetic, public and private, the house defines a new threshold. It is a threshold that seeks to recognise changing patterns of social behaviour and the consequent contradictions inherent in a scheme that brings together weekenders from the city and the inhabitants of a rural Indian village in an effort to integrate two different communities. ∆

House at Khim, Alibag, India, 2001

Top
Site plan.
Front elevation.

Middle
The entrance to the house showing the wall that divides the site into two zones.

Bottom
Detail of wall with staircase to the terrace.

Notes
1. Rahul Mehrotra and William Glover, 'An attitude towards conservation', *Dimensions* v15, p 69.
2. Ibid, p 71.
3. Ibid, p 73.
4. Ibid. p 73.

Arup/Arup Associates

Learning and teaching in Ladakh, a predominantly Buddhist society, were traditionally centred in the monastery. However, most of the schools in this remote region of northern India that borders on Tibet are now administered either by the Indian state system or run by other religious groups as mission schools. The majority of these schools serve the area around the town of Leh, and throughout the region facilities are oversubscribed and resources limited.

As a consequence, a project to develop a new educational community that would focus on the particular needs in Ladakh was initiated in 1994 by the Drukpa Kargyud Trust under the patronage of His Holiness the Dalai Lama. With the laying of a foundation stone in 1996, the initiative led to the construction of a school designed to foster the development of a curriculum integrating modern academic education, Buddhist principles and the practical needs of the developing local community.

In this ancient kingdom located high in the western Himalayas, the site for the school is in the village of Shey on the main road through central Ladakh. Situated in the Indus River

valley more than 3500 metres above sea level, this is a dry, mountainous area in a seismic region that is arid in summer and frequently cut off by snow for many months of the year. However, although winter temperatures can drop as low as −30˚C, the sky is often clear and the rich fertile valleys are warmed by the sun. It is a place that of necessity has become self-sufficient over the centuries yet at the same time also benefited from being at the crossroads of the Silk Route and the Salt Road.

The proposal to develop the new school was a direct response to requests from community elders who could see the fabric of their society beginning to disintegrate under the pressures of modernisation. The Drukpa Kargyud Trust, a UK-registered charity, worked closely with His Holiness the 12th Gyalwang Drukpa, the head of the Drukpa Kargyud School of Tibetan Buddhism. However, to develop the design the trust also sought the assistance of a multidisciplinary team. Working with Arup and Arup Associates, its proposal takes account of the exceptional circumstances in this remote place and incorporates appropriate technology using some of the most highly developed technological skills in the world.

As a fundamental part of the process a master plan projected over a 12-year period was established to serve the overall educational needs of the community. The plan addressed the critical issues of resources, climate and the declared educational objectives, and included a phased building programme for a co-educational population of 750 students ranging in age from 3 to 18 years, with an eventual capacity of 850. The scheme will provide education from kindergarten and nursery school through secondary education and vocational training, together with computer laboratories, studios and workshops, a medical clinic, an open-air temple, a farm with cottage gardens, and residential accommodation for up to 200 pupils and staff.

The whole project has been conceived as a model for appropriate and sustainable modernisation in Ladakh, and the school is recognisable as a constructed figure that is clearly identifiable in the expansive natural setting. The overall plan has been developed to take maximum advantage of the site with a single-storey complex orientated along a north–south axis and facing south. The buildings are cut into the ground for shelter and warmth and the forms of the school have been developed following studies of local materials, construction techniques and vernacular buildings including the monasteries that have evolved complex and sophisticated architectural forms.

Water is a limited resource here and its conservation has been a major influence in shaping development in the region. For example, within the traditional communities there are distinct riparian

Druk White School, Ladakh, 2002

Opposite, top left
Plan of the kindergarten.

Opposite, top right
CFD plan of solar-assisted VIP latrines

Opposite, bottom left
The master plan for the new school has been developed within the framework of the mandala.

Opposite, bottom right
Solar-assisted VIP latrines.

Below
The external courtyard provides outdoor play space and secure teaching areas for pupils at the school.

'The idea of having a modern school which lays equal emphasis on the importance of preserving the valuable aspects of a traditional culture is very encouraging… I have always believed in giving equal importance to both modern, scientific knowledge and traditional Buddhist culture.' — His Holiness the 14th Dalai Lama

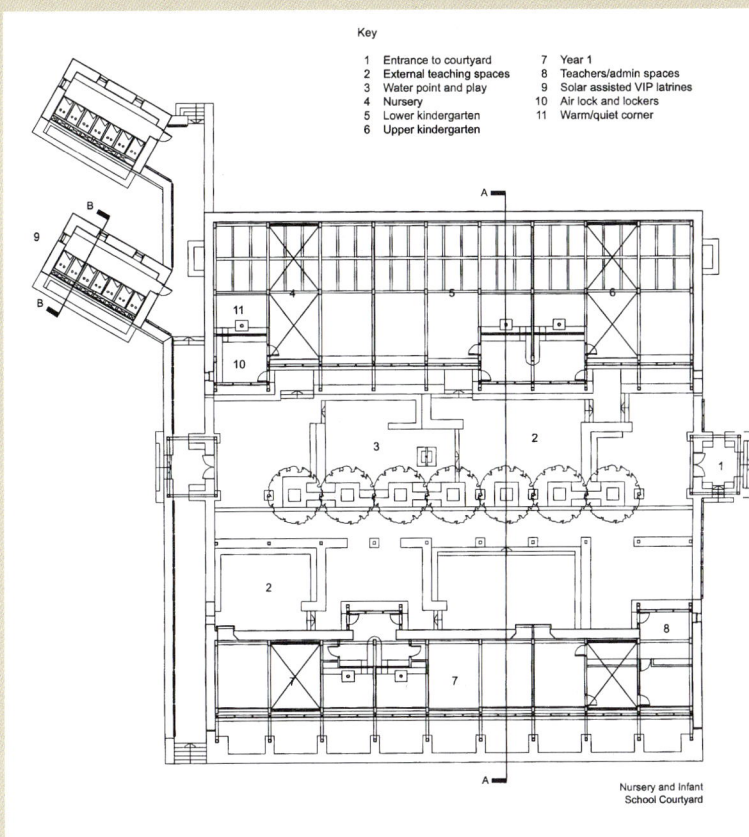

Key

1	Entrance to courtyard	7	Year 1
2	External teaching spaces	8	Teachers/admin spaces
3	Water point and play	9	Solar assisted VIP latrines
4	Nursery	10	Air lock and lockers
5	Lower kindergarten	11	Warm/quiet corner
6	Upper kindergarten		

Nursery and Infant
School Courtyard

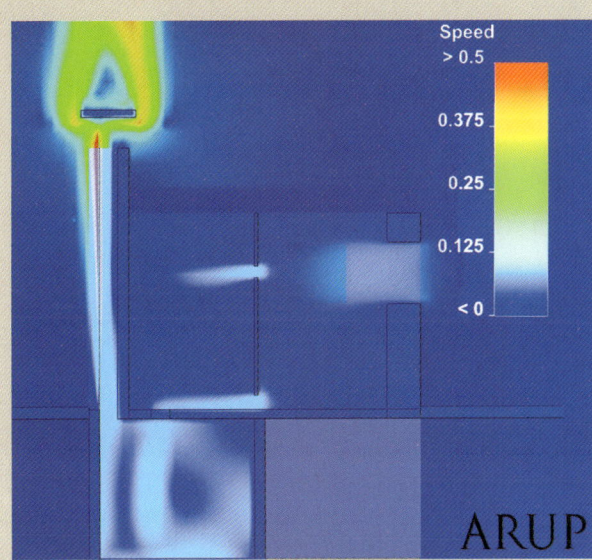

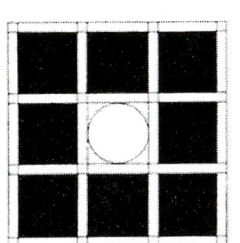

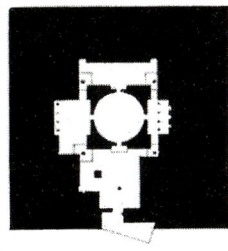

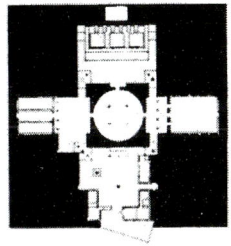

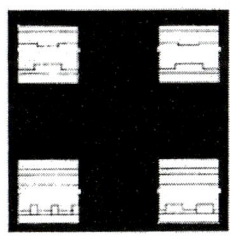

rights that limit the amount of water that can be used for irrigation, and this system is clearly imprinted on the landscape by the networks of water channels defining land-holdings. Learning from the existing landscapes, the plan for the school creates a water distribution system that is also clearly readable on the site. Ground water is pumped by solar power to a tank at the northern boundary of the site, and the main water supply is routed along the north–south axis of the development. The system also reuses water for irrigation and directs the small amount of rainfall to planted areas. The distribution system forms the spine of the development and defines a series of sites for the home-farm gardens, residential accommodation and the school itself.

Other influences for the school include those rooted in the sociocultural traditions of the place rather than those derived from characteristics of the physical environment. The eight-spoked dharma wheel, which represents Buddhist teachings, and the nine-square mandala, which symbolises the inner and outer worlds of the subjective and objective realms, are reflected in the organisation of spaces. The dharma wheel, at its simplest level, is a circular figure with eight spokes radiating from its centre. Within the plan for the school, this forms the basis for a central temple and assembly courtyard designed as a hall space with eight openings. Four of these are entrances planned on the cardinal points and four lead into shrine rooms. Together with the figure of the mandala, the two patterns form an underlying structure for the school.

In a traditional nine-square grid surrounded by a series of concentric circles, the school buildings have been sited in each of the four corners of the figure. The outer rings are formed by low walls, eight stupas and 32 willow trees. Within the overall structure of this plan, the school now in use represents an eighth of the educational complex.

All of the buildings have been designed using materials that take advantage of the high-altitude climate and optimise beneficial sunshine, shading, insulation and natural ventilation for cooling and fresh air. The school generates its own energy and exports no waste. It reduces local emissions by the use of solar panels that maximise Ladakh's consistent exposure to direct sun to feed battery packs in an energy centre that provides basic lighting outside of daylight hours and powers the water supply, school equipment and computers.

A series of composting toilets use solar-powered stacks. Here, the solar energy, collected in black south-facing walls, heats a duct that draws air through the latrines and expels it up through the duct above roof

level, avoiding flies and odours, and double chambers within these specially designed ventilated pit latrines allow waste to be converted for use as fertiliser every other year.

The nursery and infant school opened in September 2001 and consists of a series of classrooms and staff offices grouped around an open courtyard that provides secure outdoor teaching spaces. Designed to make the maximum use of indigenous materials, the timber-framed buildings are enclosed by stone walls. One of the main challenges for the design team was to learn from and also improve traditional construction systems. The heavy timber frames, made from fir imported from renewable sources, act as an integral part of the structure of the building and help to resist earthquake forces. The rafters and infill between them are willow, obtained locally from plantations, which forms the support for an earth roof. Also brought from local sources this earth was layered and compacted by the villagers who gave their time as a contribution to the project.

The stone is also obtained locally and, though more expensive than the mud that is more frequently used for building in Ladakh, here it not only signifies the importance of the new building but also helps to conserve valuable soil for agricultural use.

The second stage of the project, which includes a junior school, residential courtyard, dining hall and kitchens, is currently under construction and is scheduled for completion in 2004. Since the Arup design team was invited to help the Drukpa Kargyud Trust, it has been working on the project on a semi-voluntary basis. A member of Arup's staff has been resident on site during each summer building season and together with multidisciplinary groups in Arup's offices in London and Japan has helped to develop and test both the design and approach to construction.

The Ladakh project clearly demonstrates the value of enlightened and sustained international collaboration, and has been described by Arup Associates' architect Jonathan Rose as 'an example of how design can not only symbolically and physically support a cause but also maintain local tradition and culture. The Druk White School project offers an example of appropriate modernisation and a sustainable model for other communities and cultures in the world that are under enormous pressure to change'. ∆ BC

Druk White School, Ladakh, 2002

Opposite
The construction of the school entailed the erection of heavy timber frames on which willow poles were placed.
A secondary layer of willow sticks created a base for the laying of mud and grass coverings with a sacrificial topping of mud to finish off the roof.

Right, top
Classrooms have been designed to maximise the use of natural light and provide good views out to the courtyard.

Right, middle
Interior of one of the kindergarten classrooms, showing the heavy timber-frame construction.

Right, bottom
The school is built using local granite so as to avoid using valuable soil that is often employed in stabilised earth construction.

Guinea in West Africa is at the core of the entire continent's ecosystem. On the Atlantic coast, it has the sources of Africa's largest rivers – the Niger, Senegal and Gambia. Employing building materials that do not contribute to deforestation and erosion, as well as developing local skills and crafts, are all priorities.

Heikkinen-Komonen

Over the last 15 years, the Indigo Foundation, a Finnish development association, has directed a series of small-scale education programmes in Africa. Under the leadership of its founder Eila Kivekas, the foundation first assisted the development of poultry farming and subsequently expanded to include nutrition programmes and the provision of vocational training for women.

All of the projects have been initiated in Guinea, and as an integral part of its evolving educational programmes the foundation has overseen the design and construction of a series of innovative new buildings. As these schemes were organised to improve local educational standards, so the Finnish architects Heikkinen-Komonen, who designed the buildings, developed projects that would not only extend the skills and capabilities of local craftspeople and builders but also be sensitive to the natural environment of this particular part of West Africa.

Villa Eila

The town of Mali, where several of the projects have been built, is the centre of the local prefecture. Located in the uplands of Fouta Djalon in the northern part of Guinea it is close to Mount Tangue, one of the highest mountains in the region. The Villa Eila was built on the outskirts of the town in 1995. Constructed on a west-facing tiled platform terraced with stone walls, bushes and fruit trees, the modest house consists of a series of inward-looking individual rooms that define open spaces in between, which in turn open out to provide views to the surrounding mountains. Planned under a single large roof, the rooms are screened from the light of the sun by woven bamboo.

Although brick-burning and burnt-over clearing for cultivation are still common in Guinea, both have now been made illegal as they contribute to deforestation and erosion – factors that constitute a serious threat to the ecosystem. As a result the majority of the buildings that have been designed here for the Indigo Foundation use stabilised earth construction. Heikkinen-Komonen adopted this way of building, which is traditional in West Africa, in order to minimise the use of burned brick. This also reduces the importation of building materials and limits the need for heavy transport.

The raw material used for stabilised earth construction is available almost everywhere, and while the places where it is excavated must be carefully selected to avoid the loss of valuable agricultural soil, it presents an inexpensive environmentally appropriate way of building. Consequently the design and construction of these new buildings protects the local landscape and economy. With the sources of three of Africa's largest

Villa Eila, Mali, 1995

Below, left
View of elevation.

Below, right
Ground-floor plan and section.

rivers – the Niger, Senegal and Gambia – in the area, it is also an approach that helps to maintain the balance of natural systems across the region.

Stabilised earth construction involves the combination of a small amount of cement with moistened earth. This mix is formed into building blocks that are hardened not by firing but with a manual press – a technique that with the addition of a little more cement and sisal fibre in the mix can also be used to make floor and roof tiles. The blocks work well in compression and their high thermal capacity enables them to store heat during the day and retain the coolness from the night air.

Although the various projects have been developed to utilise similar materials and methods of construction, they explore different site-planning strategies. Several are public rather than private buildings, including a health centre built in 1994 and two elementary schools constructed in the villages of Boundou Koura and Madina Kouta three years later. Planned as a series of individual buildings that were small and easy to build, these schemes have been planned to define new civic spaces where families can meet and children can gather.

Poultry School

The most recent project, a school for poultry farmers developed as a part of the Kahere poultry station near the town of Kindia, is south of Mali.

Located about 100 kilometres northeast of the capital Conakry, it is a development of 350 square metres that includes a classroom and accommodation for 12 students with an office, a house for a teacher and a water-storage tower. The school is planned within four separate buildings that have been grouped to enclose a square courtyard.

In previous projects, the load-bearing stabilised earth block walls were constructed with a single brick thickness so as to save material. However, in this scheme the wall thickness has been increased by using

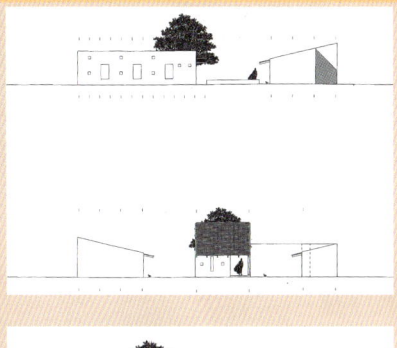

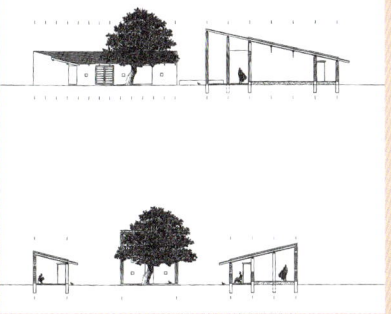

Poultry School, Kindia, 1999

Above right
North, south, east and west elevations.

Right
The school has been planned to create a defined compound in the lush jungle of Guinea.

a double-skin construction that not only improves the building's thermal performance but also obviates the need for additional reinforcement. Within the walls, the windows and openings have been carefully placed to encourage natural ventilation. In addition, many openings do not exceed 30 centimetres in width and can be supported by bonded masonry and without lintels. Roofs are simple mono-pitches that use only small-section lumber and in places are partially reinforced with steel trusses.

This modest group of new buildings represents a significant addition to the educational programmes in this region of Guinea. Through the thoughtfulness of its planning the new school, denoted by a public square, generous shaded verandah and intense splash of cobalt blue, also establishes the value of design in the founding of a significant public institution. ᗡ BC

Poultry School, Kindia, 1999

Above
The classroom has been designed with a generous porch overlooking the school courtyard.

Right
Ground-floor plan.

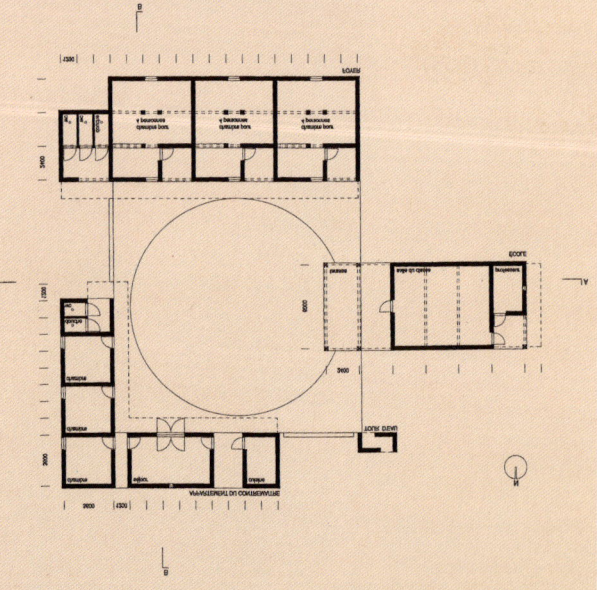

Geographically, Chile is both one of the most attenuated and isolated nations on earth. Almost 4000 kilometres long – equivalent to the distance from Scotland to Nigeria – it is a country that is on average only 120 kilometres wide. Although now connected by the north–south line of the Pan-American Highway and an efficient system of air travel, the geographical and climatic regions of Chile are still distinctly different realms – from the Altiplano in the northern Andes to rich agricultural land around Santiago, temperate rain forests in the lake district and barren windswept islands close to Antarctica.

Chile is separated from Argentina to the east by the formidable wall of the Andes, and from Peru and Bolivia to the north by the inhospitable Atacama Desert. Only a few islands dot the vast Pacific Ocean between Chile and New Zealand, its nearest neighbour to the west.

This has created a distinct physical and psychological context for architecture. The indigenous peoples of Chile, unlike the Incas and Mayas to the north, were warriors rather than builders. Under Spanish colonial rule, Chile was administered as a poor outpost of their Peruvian colony. And because of the country's location along a major geological fault line, such historic building stock that did exist has been largely destroyed over the centuries by frequent earthquakes.

In recent years, Chile's economic and political fortunes have been mixed. When the socialist government of Salvador Allende was toppled by a military coup in 1973, power was assumed by General Agosto Pinochet. Although Pinochet rescued an economy in chaos by imposing strict principles of free-market capitalism, his regime was harsh and repressive. When the government fell in 1988, Chile emerged as a democracy savouring its new freedoms.

Geography, a lack of architectural nostalgia for the past, cultural and economic ties to Europe and North America, and this particular moment in its political evolution have contributed to the 'flowering' of a lively debate that, more than in any other Latin American country, can be seen in a diverse range of outstanding contemporary Chilean architecture.

'Plenitude, Time and the Emptiness of Space'

German del Sol

German del Sol explains how, after over a decade of practising abroad in Spain and the United States, he chose to return home to work in his native Chile, where he has explored the expansiveness of landscape, time and space.

In Chile we live as if on an island. Because the architectural community is small and relatively isolated, we coexist locally in an atmosphere of entente cordiale. It is therefore important that we expose ourselves and our work to the outside world. For 10 years I lived in Spain, where I studied architecture, before spending two-and-a-half years in California. When I returned I decided to work in remote places to attract people to Chile. These are places in which there are no patrons and no cities. What we have to offer instead is plenitude, time and the emptiness of space.

The concept of Explora is to design hotels in remote places that encourage people to be like children, to go outside and play. This kind of outdoor life has no goals such as 'exercise' or 'fitness'. Its purpose is pleasure, in the sense that outdoor life is good for the spirit. At Explora, the rituals of the day invite people to be quiet. Like the movement of the sea or the flames of a fire, we are interested in movement without direction or goal that nonetheless invites you to stop and look. Explora places you in a context that takes you outside yourself. I got involved with Explora as a partner because I did not believe anyone would ever ask me to do such a project. Two of the hotels have already been built, the first in Patagonia at the southern tip of Chile and the second in the Atacama Desert to the north. Now, because people around the world are aware of and enthusiastic about Explora, the environment that we have created is in some sense protected. The other sites we have in mind are on the island of Chiloe, in the central valley of Chile and in the Altiplano.

As an architect, I am accustomed to resistance. Everything new must be resisted. If I do not find this friction, then something is wrong. Resistance is a means of checking the freshness and vitality of the idea. When we proposed the Explora hotels, people in Patagonia and the Atacama resisted because they thought it would threaten their businesses. To the contrary these hotels have raised the level of interest in these remote places. The Explora concept acknowledges that people want to travel in many ways. Its concept of hospitality is not one that reflects upon the host. It is a more delicate, more refined, more educated approach to tourism that focuses on the silence, vastness and space of nature.

I wanted to make a hotel in the wilderness without all of the usual *mise en scène*. The original idea of Explora was very basic: to provide a counterpoint between being in nature and returning to a comforting refuge. In the Atacama, the hotel is just outside the existing town of San Pedro and is like a small town itself. It is a complex, not a building. The municipality was against the design of the hotel; they wanted us to make something that looked like a Spanish building. Instead, my models were Frank Lloyd Wright's Ocotillo Camp and Le Corbusier's hut on Lake Geneva –

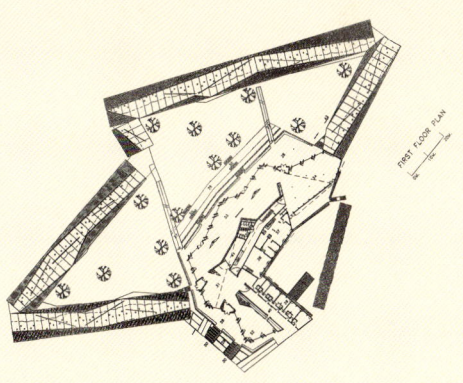

Hotel San Pedro de Atacama,
1999

Right
Site plan.

Far right, top
Ground-floor plan.

Far right, bottom
First-floor plan.

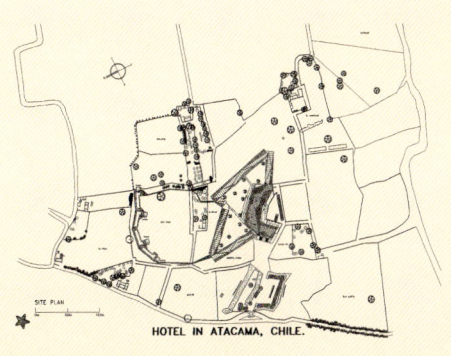

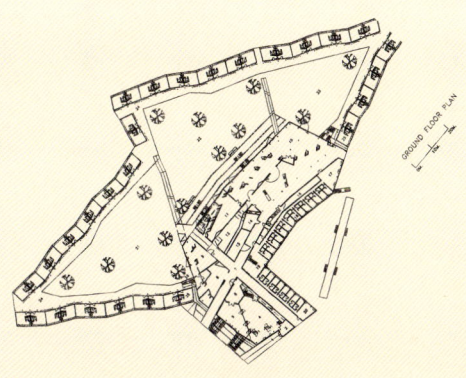

All life in the Atacama is gathered around water. Like other settlements, the hotel at San Pedro is an oasis. Starting with architecture and the plaza, we make a connection with the landscape with a line of still water. Instead of one large swimming pool, which would be quite foreign to the place, we made four pools.

The custom in Chile is to saddle up and to keep the horses tethered while they are waiting to be ridden. In the desert, the waiting horse must have shade and water. A wooden shading structure wraps the inner edge of the stable plaza, complemented by a long trough of still water.

buildings that go back to the beginning, using materials in a primitive way to make a modern place. This is the same thing that Richard Long does with his sculpture. In his hands, a circle of stones becomes something sophisticated. Like Richard Long, we try to do much with minimal means. The relationship between one person and another is not based on physical similarities. Man and wife do not look alike, but rather share love. A hotel in the Atacama does not have to look like the old buildings in the desert but instead must follow the spirit of the place.

The hotel draws upon the simple ways of life in the desert. People who live in the Atacama have the most beautiful textiles in the world yet they live in simple mud houses. All of the houses, like horses at the racecourse, are marked with coloured wood. While the houses are quite rough, the textiles, clothes and furniture – the things people touch – are very sophisticated. In thinking about a hotel in this context, it is critical to understand that not everything is important. Without mockery, we built the Explora Hotel at San Pedro de Atacama without worrying too much about the quality of workmanship – that is, the wood and concrete are not precise.

I lived one week per month in both Patagonia and the Atacama before building there. Each project took five years. In the Atacama I went to talk to the owner of the land near San Pedro on which we wanted to site the hotel. I asked for a tape measure and he replied: 'The tape measure is very imprecise'. In his mind, the land is a 'cuerpo cierto', a body determined not by dimensions but by its character. Part of the Explora concept is that the surrounding natural and cultural environment has to be preserved. In Patagonia, the mountains and lakes are near to the hotel. In the Atacama, they are distant. To emphasise this, the hotel there is built around an empty plaza. Our model was the Mayan city. In the middle of nowhere, instead of building streets first, the Mayans built a flat platform to contrast with the imprecise land. They then placed buildings on it, related not by streets but by their presence on the platform. Using this model at San Pedro, the main building forms the heart of the plaza and the bedrooms define the edge against the vastness of the desert.

As architects we have artistic rather than scientific certitudes. I have an idea that all lines in the Atacama are made by walls of mud or river stone, which are more like hedgerows than straight lines of barbed wire or wood fences. This produces a setting with a different kind of

precision – a beautiful imprecision. The ideas, the certitudes, are not imposed from outside but grow out of the land. We bought several properties, and mindful of the character of the land kept the mud walls that had been built around the edges of each field. In contrast with the colonial way of building cities, the forms of the hotel arise from the centuries-old boundaries of the fields.

***

We wanted to build our own horizon. When standing or sitting in the main building, the bedroom roofs are at eye level. Everything below this new horizon is the hotel, and everything above is the Atacama.

***

The hotel at San Pedro is a public building that is different from, say, a group of houses. The main building is on a three-metre-high platform while the surrounding bedrooms are raised just one-and-a-half metres above the ground. Because the bedrooms are slightly elevated, people can tend the crops and livestock in the fields without disrupting the privacy of the hotel guests in their rooms. We wanted to build our own horizon. When standing or sitting in the main building, the bedroom roofs are at eye level. Everything below this new horizon is the hotel, and everything above is the Atacama. The bedrooms define the edge of the place of the hotel and the vastness of the desert beyond. The curved metal roofs create both a boundary in the foreground and a distant horizon. It is the same principle as at Chichen Itza, where the main buildings are elevated so that you can see over the jungle and understand your place in the world. This Mayan idea is very different from the medieval lord making a walled compound. The Mayan concept is not one of defending a last stronghold, but of keeping an eye on what is below and beyond.

The hotel has two roofs that reflect two different systems and geometries. Above the flat roofs of the buildings is a second lighter roof that creates covered walkways, shades the buildings and tempers the hot, dry climate of the desert. Locally these shading structures are typically made from several layers of branches. At the hotel they are framed by dimension lumber and clad with copper. The sun in the desert is penetrating and one is always searching for shade. Shade there is not dark, but is punctuated by light penetrating through the layers of branches. We did not want to use branches because that would have been too folkloric. We did not copy traditional forms of construction but alluded to them in another way. We revealed the layers of our construction, peeling back the copper cladding at the edges of the shading structures to expose the wood framing. Light penetrates through this 'fringe' along the edge, creating changing patterns of light and shadow as the sun and moon move through their diurnal, monthly and seasonal cycles. As you walk under this roof, instead of a dark penumbra the changing patterns of light invite you to move ahead.

This idea of working with moving light is also drawn from the vibration of intense daylight in the desert. In the same way, and thinking about the character of the place, I fought against having bright light in the hotel at night. The Atacama may well be one of the few places on earth without electric light at night. In the desert, there is only the star-filled night sky.

I could not be British, because the landscape there is too perfect. I am South American and I understand the landscape in the indigenous way. The landscape is endless. In order for wilderness to be wild, it has to be seen in contrast with ground that has some architectural marks. The hotel has no garden, but it does have a landscape. All of the fields around the hotel are irrigated – not sprinkled but flooded so that the pressure of deep water reaches deep roots. All towns in the Atacama have '*charcas*', or large pools. In some places they are in the middle of town and in others they are small lagoons around the town. There is still no running water in the desert.

All life in the Atacama is gathered around water. Like other settlements, the hotel at San Pedro is an oasis. Starting with architecture and the plaza, we make a connection with the landscape with a line of still water. Instead of one large swimming pool, which would be quite foreign to the place, we made four pools so that they could use just one at a time for irrigation. In these pools, water overflows the edges and is still. It reflects the surroundings. The pools are located at the edges of fields where trees are more abundant. The broken line of water reflects the sky, the green of the trees and the small white pavilions adjacent to the pools. Without imitating nature, we have created an abstraction of the mountains and clouds reflected in the water of the desert.

Farm buildings are beautiful because they are modest, presenting themselves simply as what

At Puritama, the footpath was designed from traces of human use of the site over centuries, not by zigzags drawn in the office.

they are and not pretending to be something else. We wanted the stables and the garage of the hotel to have a similar character, and we wanted people to see them. The stables and parking are bounded by walls of a single material, white-painted concrete. They are planned to form a second irregularly shaped plaza which forms the entrance forecourt to the hotel. In the stables, coloured, dappled light is admitted through holes in the concrete roof that are infilled with bottle glass. One hole in each stall remains open, allowing rainwater to drain where the horse does not stand. These small patches of light enliven the stables and help with cleanliness.

Because the hotel is conceived as a town, we have created deliberate ambiguity between inside and outside. Monumentally scaled doors open the foyers to the out of doors. Horses can be ridden through the main building at ground level, so guests in the public rooms above may hear the sound of the horses' hoofs on the stone pavement. There are likewise multiple paths through this 'town'. Guests can go to the dining room through the foyers, through an open-air alley at the heart of the main building or from terraces. The living room of the hotel is designed as a large empty space, the equivalent of the empty square outside, to allow for distance between people.

At the hot springs at Puritama, located in a rugged and secluded valley 15 kilometres northeast of San Pedro, the strategy is quite different. Our intervention there is more modest. We have created a raised path for visitors to walk along the river without touching the ground. The meandering path does not impose a direction but invites movement. At Puritama, the footpath was designed from traces of human use of the site over centuries, not by zigzags drawn in the office. We retained two very old Inca stone houses and built two new white-painted concrete pavilions to house changing rooms. And we have 'built' shade. In the desert, shade makes a place even when there is nothing else. The shade structure is located where, over the years, people had camped, built fires and scarred the ground.

I do not think about Explora in the Atacama as a narrative, but as an experience of the landscape, the weather and the people without a narrative. I want

people to have the experience without being conscious of how it has been accomplished. For example, when it occasionally rains, water running off the copper roof leaves green stains on the concrete. I want to let these things happen in an open way instead of controlling the outcome like Disneyland. Most hotels want to 'soften' the entrance experience. I think that is boring. In Barcelona many restaurants are entered through the kitchens, so that you see fully the life of the place.

I do not think about Explora in the Atacama as a narrative, but as an experience of the landscape, the weather and the people without a narrative.

I intentionally made the entrance to the hotel through the stables, which are normally tucked away out of sight. I have been criticised for making the entrance stair up to the platform very steep. I did this so that you have to concentrate on ascending the stair and so that when you arrive at the top it is a surprise.

In my experience, architectural schools often promote a calculated way of thinking that strives for perfection. I do not believe in perfection. Instead, I believe in being open to what is going to happen. A mistake is often beautiful. Just as a good linen shirt is always wrinkled, so the workers in the Atacama cannot build the perfect wall. Walls gather dust and develop cracks over time. More important than perfection is the idea that beauty appears through ageing. We work with, rather than against, that idea. Form has to follow life. Architecture must follow, instead of imposing or leading; it must make life possible.

From conversations of German del Sol with Annette LeCuyer and Brian Carter, March 2002.

The hot springs at Puritama, 2000.

Felipe Assadi

Felipe Assadi is a member of an informal group that has been dubbed Generation 90 – young Chilean architects who have come of age during the last decade, benefiting from Chile's flourishing economy and growing political freedom. In addition to designing and building, Assadi's architectural voice is also heard through weekly articles on architecture, landscape, planning and design for *El Mercurio*, a leading national newspaper.

While private houses are often the principal means by which young architects establish their reputations, two less conventional commissions reveal Assadi's skill at transforming the mundane into architectural currency. Both are simple sheds that, although quite different in context, scale and material, share much common ground.

Fruit Shed at the Schmitz House

The first project is an outbuilding for the Schmitz House, a villa designed by Assadi and completed in 2001, which is located at Calera de Tango about 60 miles from Santiago. Sited in the midst of a 4.5-hectare orchard that produces fruit and nuts, the villa is not only a sophisticated rural retreat but also the focus of a working agricultural enterprise. Responding to the need for storage of produce from the orchards, Assadi has designed a modest wooden box. Located near the entrance to the property, the slender building helps to define the boundary to the road.

Designed to suit the module of both the fruit crates to be stored within the shed and the lumber from which it is made, the building is 2.4 metres high and 1.2 metres wide by 12 metres long. Although it reads as a singular volume, it is made up of a series of discrete compartments planned on the 1.2-meter module. The long east elevation of the shed, which faces the orchards, is composed entirely of lockable doors that fully occupy each module, providing both security and ease of access into the individual storage units. The light wood frame of the building is lined internally with oriented strand board and clad externally with plywood and a slatted wood rain-screen.

Cross-ventilation in each compartment is provided by the slatted doors, which are backed with metal mesh, and by openings in the rear wall. The rear vents are consistent in size and placed at high level, reinforcing the regular rhythm of the module. In contrast, the vents in the doors – created by omitting either whole or half slats – are predominantly at low level and randomly dispersed to create an irregular counterpoint to the module. The floor of the shed is raised above the ground by a slim recessed plinth. All ironmongery is concealed, and the framing and backup wall are painted black so that the slats appear to be suspended in space.

Simply detailed, this storage building exhibits both the unpretentious workmanlike character of the fruit crates themselves and the abstraction of a minimalist installation in the ordered landscape of the orchard.

Arauco Express

The second shed, designed jointly by Felipe Assadi and Francisca Pulido, could not be more different from the fruit store. Located in the heart of Santiago, it is sited along Avenida Kennedy, a major route through the city. Instead of an orchard, it is placed in the ordered cityscape of the car park for the vast Arauco shopping mall. Instead of storage, its purpose is the rapid transfer of goods. The project, won by Assadi and Pulido in a limited competition, is an

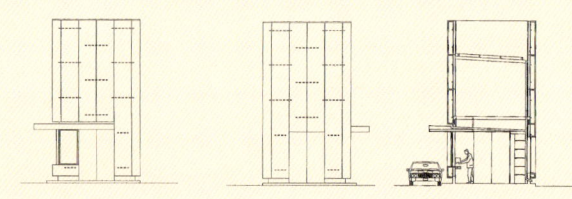

Arauco Express, Santiago, 2001

Previous page and above
The collection building for Arauco Express creates an emphatic landmark in an otherwise undifferentiated sea of car parking.

Above, right
North elevation, south elevation and cross section.

express pick-up facility for online shoppers who do not want to deal with crowds at the mall. Planned on a one-metre module, the building is eight metres high and four metres wide by 15 metres long. Organised as a two-storey volume to enhance its presence, the building is placed perpendicular to the road so that its long east and west faces, like billboards, have maximum exposure to passing vehicles.

Arauco Express essentially functions as a traffic island, with vehicles approaching along the length of its west face and looping around the pavilion to drive-up service windows on the east facade. Shoppers confirm the details of their orders to attendants at the windows, who then collect the goods from numbered storage cupboards planned in a metre-thick zone at the rear of the space. Staff-support facilities and a stair up to second-floor storage space are also housed in this thick western wall.

Like any shed, the character of Arauco Express resides principally in its skin. This steel-framed pavilion has a double skin comprising an outer layer of translucent polycarbonate that is spaced 600 millimetres away from the white-painted composite wood-panel backup wall. Between the two skins, 150 blue fluorescent lights bring this mute volume to life. In contrast with the strong vertical lines generated by the secondary framing that carries the polycarbonate, the lighting tubes are placed in alternating horizontal rows, giving the skin of the building a three-dimensional textile character. While this lighted fabric is in itself static – the lights do not blink or change colour – the skin is animated at night by multicoloured lines of light from passing vehicles, which are reflected in the polycarbonate. Using modest means, this small building is imbued with a street presence that is far greater than its actual scale. The blue box of Arauco Express has become a new landmark in the city.

Both of these simple sheds are carefully considered without being precious. Each has a distinct character – one a quiet and measured reflection upon a rural way of life, and the other a slick, sophisticated promotion of shopping in the city. In addition to drawing out the special qualities of their place and programme, they are the work of architects whose thinking is also attuned to the current international interest in minimalism and the preoccupation with the building skin.

Jose Cruz Ovalle

Recent work by Jose Cruz Ovalle focuses on discovering the potential of wood. Cruz has become an advocate for wood because it is inherently elastic, an important material property for buildings located in an active seismic zone. In Cruz's hands, this flexibility also permits formal freedom – a freedom that was exploited particularly skilfully in the design of the Chilean Pavilion for the 1992 Seville Expo where, liberated from strict orthogonal geometry, he used wood to make complex soft and sensual forms.

Unlike many architects whose current explorations of the curvilinear are digitally inspired, Cruz's motivation springs from a different source. Although he was not directly involved in the experimental Open City at Ritoque that was founded on the coast near Valparaiso some 40 years ago by architects, writers, musicians and philosophers, Cruz shares many of the same concerns. Chief among these is an interest in the experiential qualities of architecture.

Forest Industry Headquarters
During the past century, large areas of Chile's indigenous forests were cleared and systematically replanted with more profitable foreign species such as radiata pine, which grows much faster in its adopted environment than in its native California. This import has ironically become one of the most commercially important renewable resources in Chile. The country's

Forest Industry Headquarters is charged with managing the planting of radiata pine throughout Chile and its marketing worldwide. The requirement to provide management offices for this corporation together with industrial production space for wood products was an ideal commission for Cruz.

The combined headquarters and factory is located at the northern edge of Santiago on a flat site adjacent to the Pan-American Highway. This major artery, which extends from Chile's northern border with Peru to Chiloe in the south, is prime frontage for commercial and industrial development. While much of the roadside architecture here is unremarkable in character, the Forest Industry Headquarters has a strong presence. The building, an efficient box in plan, is manipulated in section. The roof is shaped into a sinuous, asymmetrical curve that is intended to create a streamlined profile that can be appreciated when travelling at speed along the highway. However, more than merely a gestural move, this form is also practical. Shaped to allow hot air to rise naturally and to be exhausted at the north and south ends of the

building, it also collects rainwater at the low point near the centre where it is directly drained away.

Management offices are planned on a mezzanine along the north face of the building with both exterior views and, within the building, an overview of the shop floor. Several years after the building was completed, requirements for increased office space prompted the need for a second building, also designed by Cruz. These new offices are organised as a single-storey bar parallel to the original building. Raised on glue-laminated piloti, and with grade parking tucked underneath, they are connected to the factory by a bridge.

To exaggerate the length of the curved roof, the primary structure runs north to south, parallel to the highway. Pairs of curved glue-laminated beams are supported by V-shaped columns which, like trees, branch out from a

single trunk. The curved profile of both columns and beams emphasises the elastic character of wood. At the north and south ends of the building, the paired beams taper to a single member, which is in turn supported by paired columns. At these locations, the inner face of the columns is straight and vertical to accommodate the exterior envelope, and the implied movement of the structure is expressed by a tapered exterior profile and wood gussets that soften the transition from beam to wall.

In contrast with the muscular sections of the timber structure, the envelope is of finely grained tongue-and-groove wood siding. While the east elevation is opaque to provide a buffer against the noise of the adjacent highway, the west facade facing the factory yard has extensive glazing. In addition, daylight on the factory floor is provided by rooflights and a system of clerestories to the north and south that are shaded by both the overhanging roof and external wood screens. In this project, the clear hierarchy of scale creates a sense of what Cruz calls 'light spatiality', which provides protection and orientation without imposing the weight of an excessive formal presence.

Perez Cruz Winery
The experiential potential of the profile, touch and smell of wood and the immaculately executed details of its

Above
**Perez Cruz Winery, Santiago,
2001**

connections has been further developed by Cruz in a recently completed winery. The central valley, which extends to the south from Santiago, is the primary agricultural region of Chile. Rich soil and a mild climate provide ideal conditions for growing grapes, with centuries-old vineyards and wineries gathered around large family estates. The Perez Cruz winery is 50 kilometres south of Santiago on a 530-hectare estate.

The new building is located at a pivotal point in the landscape which marks the transition from the expansive cultivated valley to the west to the virgin forests of the foothills of the Andes to the east, and its design takes account of the long-established building traditions of the region. Unlike the conventions of the city, farm buildings here tend not to have clearly defined fronts and backs. This is because, under the vast open sky of Chile, shade is the first – and in rural areas often the only – requirement for inhabitation. Buildings consequently have inhabited perimeters that in addition to providing protection from both sun and rain create a thick transitional zone between the full sunlight outside and cool, dark interiors.

With this tradition in mind, the winery is defined by two separate but related structures. Interior space is described by two parallel

semicircular vaults framed by glue-laminated timber arches. These arches, which span 14 metres, spring from a 1.2-metre-high reinforced concrete wall that is clad externally with dry field stone to make a rusticated base for the building. The exterior layer of enclosure is defined by the timber-framed overhanging roof supported by props extending from the arches and, at the edges, by sinuous glue-laminated columns. The space between the roof and the vaults becomes a thick inhabited zone that creates covered walkways around the perimeter. In addition, a high-level walkway in the poche between the two vaults forms a central spine of circulation that extends the length of the building to connect offices, laboratories and staff amenities at mezzanine level and provide views into the double-height tank rooms and barrel stores.

As in the Forest Industry Headquarters, the primary timber structure of the winery is substantial in section, and the building envelope is clearly differentiated by the use of small sections of wood. In places, the cladding is detailed to create a dense, opaque envelope and in others a delicate translucent skin. This dual character is brought into focus in the rooflights. Treated as voids that have been carved out of the apparently thick poche, they are lined with wood slats that diffuse daylight, suggesting instead the sense of a lightweight enclosure.

The paired vaults, which allow for parallel simultaneous winemaking operations, are broken into

Perez Cruz Winery, Santiago, 2001

Above and right
The Perez Cruz Winery is a series of timber buildings linked by an oversailing timber roof.

three discrete volumes that provide for sequential operations. All are linked by the continuity of the roof. Covered outdoor patios between the linked pavilions provide for vehicular access to the barrel and bottle stores and to the tank rooms. In addition, the high-level central walkway expands in the spaces between buildings to provide daylit offices and laboratories. Instead of being placed in a regimented straight line, the three pavilions occupy the land in a more relaxed way, adjusting to the contours of the site. This adjustment is reflected in the framing of the roof and in the tapered plans of the covered patios, one of which opens towards the vineyard and the other towards the mountains. The shifting volumes, together with the play of light and shadow created by the interaction of the sinuous structure and the curvilinear envelope, animate the building.

This winery has provided fertile territory for Cruz's exploration of the formal and experiential potential of wood. The maturing of wine is a slow process of chemistry in which the wood of the cask plays a critical role in developing the taste and bouquet of the wine. In the same way, Cruz has used wood in this project to make a building that in its overlay of thick and thin, weight and weightlessness, and shadow and light is to be savoured through what he calls a 'prolonged gaze'. Above all, this building demonstrates Cruz's firm grasp of precision and ambiguity, terms that might equally be used to make a distinction between the carefully controlled process of making, and the rich sensory experience of enjoying both wine and architecture. ⌂ AWL

Two houses in New Zealand, Chile's neighbour to the west, demonstrate an openness that reflects their location. Fronting the ocean, each in its different way creates the lightest of shelters to make places for informal weekend living. Both Coromandel Beach and the Bay of Islands are within 150 miles of Auckland and situated at the northern extreme of North Island where it gradually narrows and eventually fragments into the ocean. The houses, located on the northeastern coast, look out to the east over the Pacific Ocean and to the International Date Line.

Coromandel Beach House,
North Island, 1999

Fearon Hay

The Coromandel Beach House

The Coromandel Beach House is situated on a site near the beach and within existing pine trees. It has been planned as a series of pavilions organised on one and two floors with three bedrooms and two bathrooms configured around an open living area. These pavilions are linked by floating roof planes. However, the extensive use of full-height glazing ensures that the house still reads as a collection of buildings that have been scattered across the site and between the trees. While a part of the house is clearly rooted to the site with horizontal slabs that extend both inside and out, other rooms hover above the undulating ground. Designed for a couple with teenage children, the beach house – with its tall concrete block towers, seemingly floating timber-box bedroom and freestanding fireplace that doubles as an outdoor shower on the reverse side – recalls the eccentricities and distinct characters that make up a family.

Coromandel Beach House, North Island, 1999

Right, top
Ground-floor plan.

Right, bottom
First-floor plan.

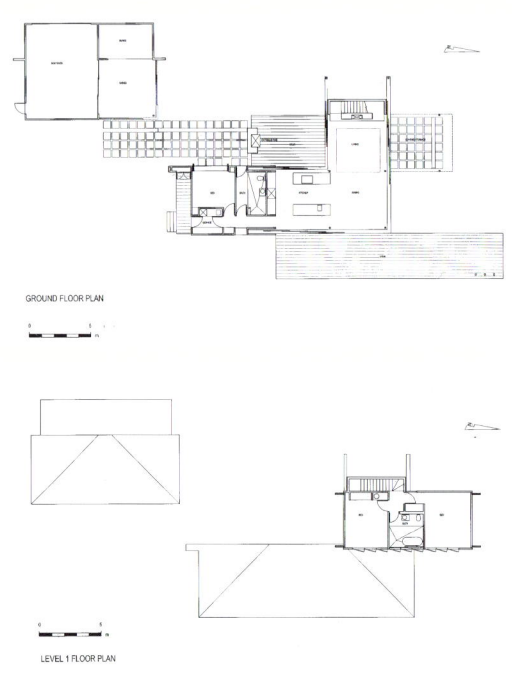

GROUND FLOOR PLAN

LEVEL 1 FLOOR PLAN

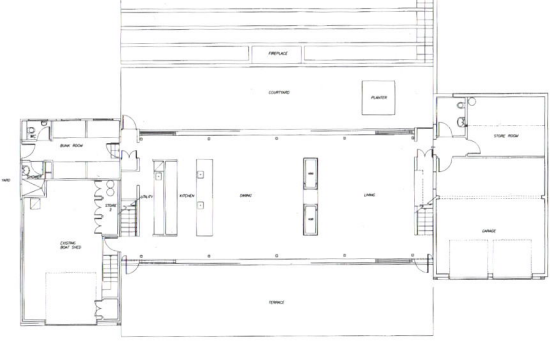

Bay of Islands House

Bay of Islands, the location of the second house, is at the foot of the Northlands Mountains near to the site of the official landing and proclamation of possession of the territory by the English in 1840. The new house is founded in the space defined by two boat sheds that already existed on the site. The archetypal form of these sheds has been enthusiastically adopted. Reclad in corrugated aluminium and louvres they form two similar dark-grey objects, scaleless and yet strangely familiar. Replanned to provide two floors of rooms, the grey sheds both emphatically define and starkly contrast with the open space between, which has been transformed with an impressive lightness to create a large single living area defined by a new floating horizontal roof. Marked only by a new masonry fireplace that projects through the roof, this is a space that is assertively open. Its fully glazed facades can be drawn back, allowing the landscape to be not merely a part of the house but to sweep completely through it. ◪ BC

Bay of Islands House, North Island, 1999

Right, top
Ground-floor plan,

Right, bottom
First-floor plan.

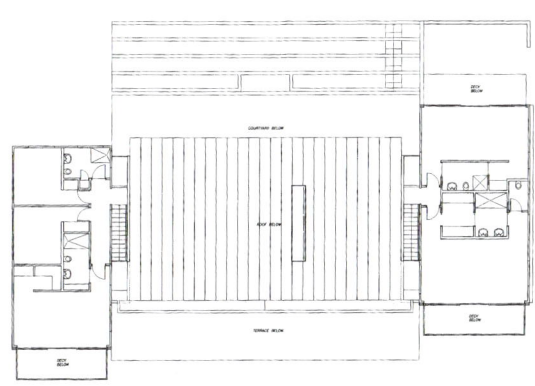

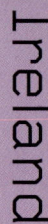

Ireland, at the extreme edge of the continent, was for many years remote from the influence of Europe. With a history rooted in a rural economy, it was also a place isolated by poverty with a population that was seemingly ever decreasing. The image of the remote thatched cottage became familiar, and with the coming of the free state and Eamon de Valera's claim that 'we are prepared to get out of the mansion, to live our lives in our own way, and to live in that frugal manner', an important part of the national identity.

The influence of that austerity, with the accompanying awareness of the importance of land, material and weather embodied in vernacular building, can still be detected in recent architecture in Ireland. However, since its entry into the European Community this architecture, like the country, is also being transformed by sweeping change. With economic improvement, private business and institutions have been revitalised while education and public services have developed, changed and expanded. The impact of European and international socioeconomic and cultural forces is suddenly obvious across Ireland in both town and country. And while the interest in things visual was so long overshadowed by the stature of the country's literary culture, Dublin and many other Irish towns and cities can now boast good examples of modern architecture and the support of newly enlightened and inspired patronage.

Three recent projects by O'Donnell + Tuomey highlight the significance of this rural history and the potential of Ireland's historic cities and institutions. The Furniture College at Letterfrack connects tradition and the new in a remote village on the west coast – a found space has been reconstructed to create a civic focus at the centre of government in the heart of Dublin's classical city – and the scheme for a new art gallery and restaurant transforms a significant riverside site and a university campus in Cork.

O'Donnell + Tuomey

The Furniture College, Letterfrack

Letterfrack village, in Connemara on the west coast of Ireland, has been the locus of three distinct phases of rural development. In the mid-19th century, a Quaker couple, John and Mary Ellis, made their way from England to this remote place and initiated a short-lived programme of construction and cultivation that introduced new readings of the landscape still clearly visible today as an overlay on the land. A number of cut-stone buildings and extensive areas of woodland survive as physical evidence of their ethical ambitions for the economic regeneration of a dejected post-famine community.

Towards the end of the 19th century, the Christian Brothers built an industrial school between the Quaker buildings and the village crossroads. The new institution was part of a nationwide programme of penal reform to provide skills training and disciplinary control for large numbers of juvenile offenders from the urban slums. The Letterfrack Reformatory closed in the 1970s. But while the cruelty that had become endemic in this system of incarceration is one of the social scandals of modern Irish society, the harsh regime of these industrial schools also brought infrastructural development to the village in the form of trade workshops and hydroelectricity. In these ways, the Christian Brothers capitalised on the earlier investment of the Quakers to continue the urbanisation of this isolated settlement.

After the Connemara West community cooperative group acquired the redundant structure from the departing Christian Brothers, a new phase of development began. The educational needs of the community were reviewed and the initiative to use this site to create a college where students could learn to design and make furniture was adopted as one of a series of local projects. The architectural brief was to draw up a framework plan that would incorporate the existing buildings, integrate new purpose-designed structures and provide for further future phases for the long-term implementation of the proposal.

When they were commissioned, the architects O'Donnell + Tuomey first considered the history of the site in order to provide a basis for the next move. Enabling works minimised demolition and the principal existing building was retained for its sound structural shell. But at the same time the architects were determined to break down the institutional self-

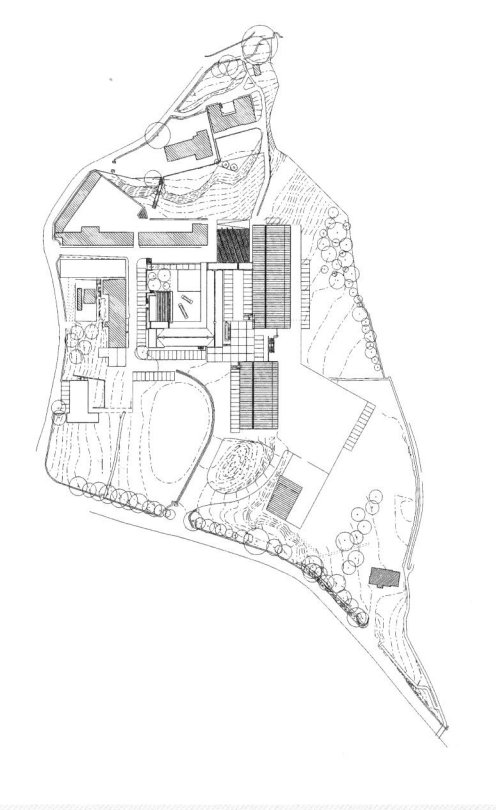

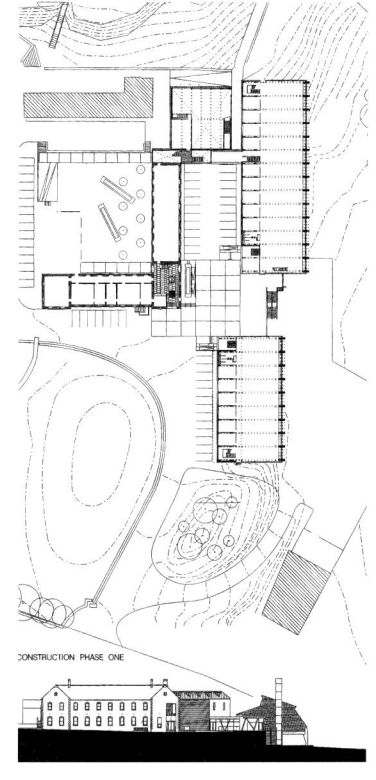

The Furniture College,
Letterfrack, 2001

Right
Master plan.

Far right
Construction phase one.

containment of the former reformatory and loosen the building's impact on the site. To do this they created a new axis of approach – a curved line in the landscape – that shifted the symmetry and connected to a new entry forecourt that opened up the closed form of the courtyard plan like a folded-out chain of spaces. Within the building itself, the spaces were replanned to eliminate corridors; windows were lowered to allow people to see out; and a new library, raised off the ground and planned over a café, was grafted onto the eastern end of the building.

Two new machine halls have been designed to front the existing buildings. Constructed on a new concrete platform, these halls have heavy timber frames consisting of flitch-plated trusses. Carefully detailed and reflecting the thoughtful construction and painstaking woodwork that is taught within the spaces, the frames are canted to create a series of clear span toplit workshops.

These workshops define one edge of a courtyard that is enclosed on the other two sides by the restored existing building and a common room and exhibition space that are currently under construction. While this space has been planned as a working courtyard, the exercise yard of the former institution defined by the two wings of existing buildings and the new library has been made into an academic garden that functions as the central social space for the college.

The effort to integrate this mix of old and new into the everyday life of both college and community will be further advanced with the completion of other later phases of development on the site. A community radio station, built onto the blind gable of the nearby community hall, is under construction, and plans to add a crèche, teaching facility and social housing will further transform the existing buildings and this remote rural setting.

The redundant reformatory was first acquired by Connemara West in the 1970s and this complex project has been developed slowly. With the completion of the machine halls, the school is in operation and students working in these spaces are currently building new furniture for the library. This in turn will become a facility within the college that will also serve as a public lending library for the village. At each stage of the work, the architects have been actively engaged not only in the design of buildings but in strategic planning and discussions of development options, materials and construction details with the founder members, shareholders and directors of Connemara West. These discussions, together with considerations of the relationships between building and landscape, and the resonance between structure and site, have formed strong foundations for the advancement of this project and the reshaping of this community on the western edge of Europe.

UCC Art Gallery

The new art gallery and restaurant at University College in Cork has been designed to provide larger and up-to-date spaces for both the college's permanent collection and changing exhibitions, as well as create a social meeting place. Located on a site close to the River Lee in the setting of the lower grounds, the organisation of this new building reflects the differing influences of site and programme.

The building is in three distinct parts. A predominantly solid, sculpted base houses the restaurant and its support spaces. By planning the restaurant within a plinth that has been shaped and projected across the site to connect the river and the existing escarpment it defines two new open spaces. One is close to the main entrance to the university and the second forms a garden green overlooking the Lee.

At the same time, the plinth provides an outdoor dining terrace with views across the green to the collegiate Gothic quadrangle, designed by Sir Thomas Deane, and to O'Donnell + Tuomey's new pedestrian bridge at Perrotts Inch that will connect the university with the city. Clad with limestone the plinth not only registers the building as a piece of the escarpment but makes it part of an ensemble of fine existing campus buildings built with the same material. Consequently it provides a conspicuous

foundation for the gallery that can be read as emerging landscape and projected building.

The gallery is planned as an interlocking suite of rooms raised up among the trees. Internally these gallery rooms are intricately interconnected in both plan and section to provide a variety of spaces at different scales and with varying lighting conditions appropriate to the exhibition of a range of different art works and artefacts. As the gallery is not conceived as a neutral white box, neither will it be hermetically sealed off from the world. Rather it has been planned as a gallery where a series of generous openings provides framed views that locate the building by the river, within the trees and as an integral part of the campus. This sculpted wooden object, lifted high above the ground, has a lightness that contrasts with the weight of the sculpted plinth. It is a contrast reinforced by a choice of materials that recalls the ephemeral form of fabric above the stereotomic platform. With a billowing oak skin that will change over time and reflect the patterns of the weather, the gallery becomes both a lookout and a series of ambiguous banners within the trees.

Restaurant and gallery are separated by an emphatic slot of space that accommodates the entrance to the building within a glassy hall and marks the intersection of a pedestrian approach from Main Avenue and a path to the riverside walk. However, this is a slot that also makes a clear distinction between platform and fabric, ground and foliage, and divides earth from sky by underlining the significance of the horizon.

Opposite
**The Furniture College,
Letterfrack, 2001**

Below
**UCC Art Gallery and
Restaurant, University
College Cork, 2002**

Sections

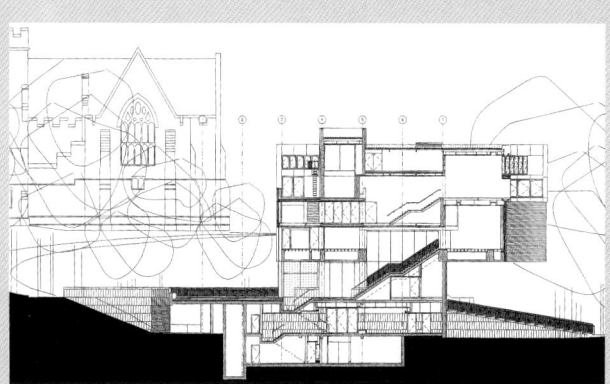

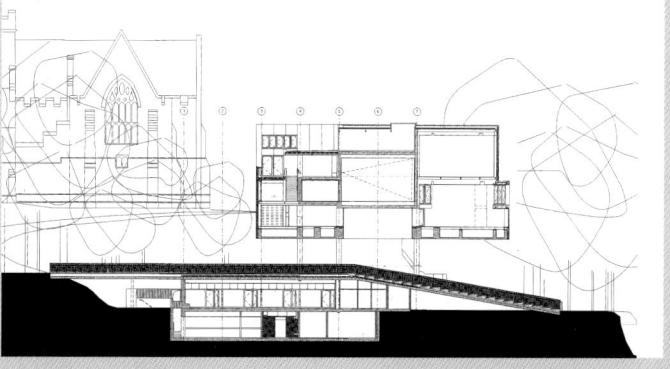

Leinster House Press Reception
Room, Dublin, 2002

Leinster House Press Reception Room

The fine buildings and spaces created in Dublin during the 18th century have left an indelible civic presence. This is clearly visible at Leinster House. Designed in 1745 by Richard Cassels as a town house for the Fitzgerald family, the stone-built Palladian-style building has remained largely unaltered. Following the Act of Union it was occupied by the Dublin Society – now the Royal Dublin Society – and under its aegis became the hub of a complex of cultural institutions. Later, in 1921, Leinster House became the home of Dail Eirann, the Irish Parliament, and located alongside several national museums provides a civilised seat of government at the heart of Dublin.

With an increasing interest in making the processes of government more transparent came the need for more public spaces in Leinster House. Among the spaces required was a place that could serve educational purposes and accommodate groups of schoolchildren visiting parliament and where members of the government could meet with special guests and the media. An examination of the existing fabric of Leinster House led to the discovery of a modest space hidden within a stair hall in the northern corner of the building. Disused but toplit, and with the potential for direct access from the house as well as the adjacent public courtyard, it was a valuable find.

Within the almost nine-metre-high volume, architects O'Donnell + Tuomey have inserted a fragment of a giant stone stair. Like a remnant of an ancient Pnyx, it is shaped in plan to suggest a bowl shape and its flush detailing emphasises the monolithic character of the stone. The series of large steps appears to have been chiselled out of a hill in a way that recalls the seat of democracy in Athens. In its plan, section and materiality this is, like those historic precedents, an architecture of theatre where citizens – whether schoolchildren, townspeople or journalists – can focus their attention on the speaker. Standing in an open space formed by a stone platform like the classical bema, and lit by daylight from the restored Georgian rooflight above, the speaker is in full view of the citizenry that he or she has been elected to serve. Like its Athenian counterpart, the design of this space seeks to hold government responsible for its words.

Within this 100-square-metre space the planning is ingenious. There is generous provision for universal access, and by making use of both plan and section an audiovisual projection room has been fitted above the stepped seating. In addition, a fully serviced television studio suite is inserted under the raked floor. With a discreetly planned entrance, this can be used at a moment's notice, either separately or together with the main space for press conferences and ministerial interviews. Rediscovered and finely made, the room provides a fine new space in Leinster House that fittingly recalls the ancient and inspiring spaces of democracy. ⚿ BC

Leinster House Press Reception Room, Dublin, 2002

Left, top
Site plan.

Left, bottom
Basement plan.

Middle
Section through stairwell.

Right
Section through entrance ramp.

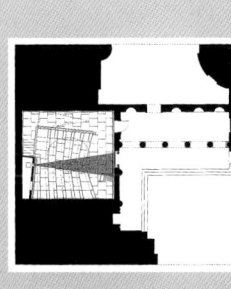

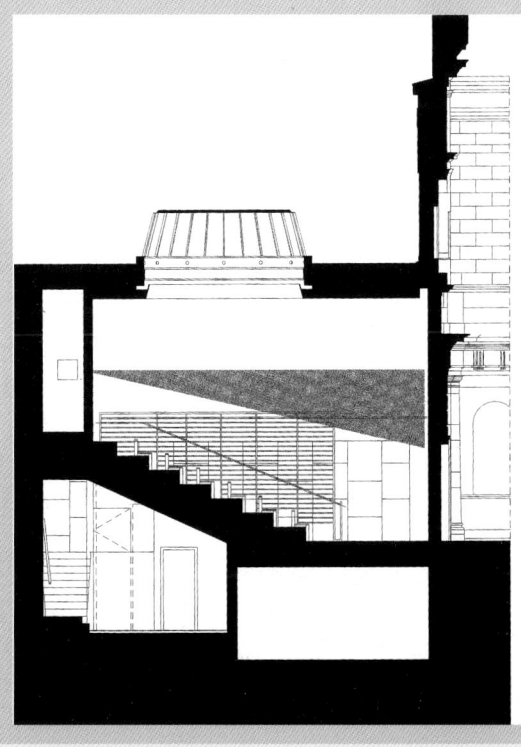

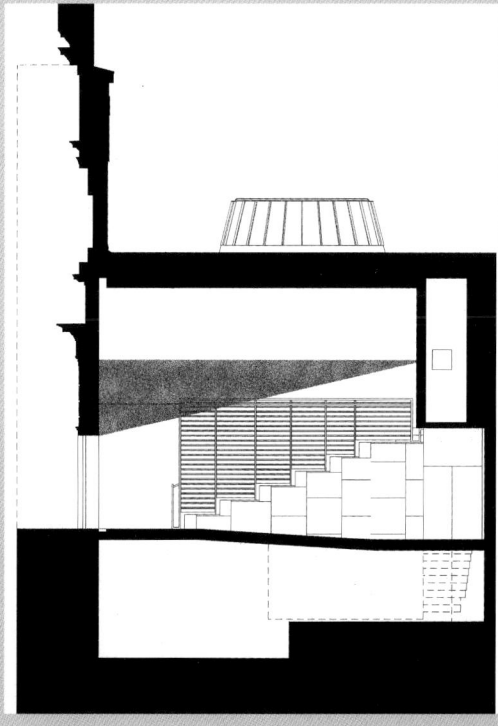

Form,
Time
and Construction

'The pace of practice taxes our patience and nothing ever seems to be finished to our satisfaction.' John Tuomey suggests a way forward out of this dilemma by finding pleasure in the process by which work is made. He advocates a recasting of the craft tradition that focuses on the integration between construction and site.

These notes are an effort to set out some principles that motivate us as architects. We always intend to start every project from the beginning and, despite years of experience, to behave as if it had never been done before. But we know there are certain constants in our thinking that provide continuity for us in our work.

We refer to cinema, topography and the traditions of architecture for inspiration more than to contemporary practice or current technologies. We look at buildings and expect them to help us understand what an architect can do in a given situation. We travel with novels in our pockets. In *Moby Dick*, Herman Melville observed: '...for small erections may be finished by their first architects; grand ones, true ones ever leave the copestone to posterity. God keep me from ever completing anything'. The pace of practice taxes our patience and nothing ever seems to be finished to our satisfaction. We have learned to take pleasure in the process by which work is made.

Form: Character, Personality and the Psychology of Function

A line drawn around an object describes its shape, and the material it is made from determines its weight. An object becomes a thing only when it is put to some sort of use, whether practical or intellectual – a hammer in the hand or a book read through at one sitting. Form, substance and appropriation by use are three components of character in architecture.

Building design, construction specification and functional planning are elements in the skills and expertise of an architect's practice, but they do not embody our sense of purpose or define an architect's role in the world. The elegant economy of a folding chair or the silence of an obelisk remembered take us closer to understanding the craft and culture of our work. Works of architecture engage the eye and the mind, the memory and the imagination in the way that fine art touches us. Yet architecture cannot be an art in the pure sense, for as Hegel reminds us it is inextricably caught up in mundane affairs. Unlike poetry or painting, architecture needs an occasion, a liturgy or an everyday event to give it resonance. 'Poetry makes nothing happen', according to Auden, but the poetics of architecture are fastened to function in the fullest sense of that value-freighted word.

When we are working we concentrate our energies on form, material and fitness for use. We express ourselves by drawing and adhering to the hand-to-eye technique by which a pencil becomes a tool of thought. 'How do I know what I think until I see what I say?' asks EM Forster. We think in material as well as spatial terms believing that the density or presence of a building is fundamentally communicated through its constructed reality.

We constantly rework our designs from concept sketch to working drawings in the conviction that the operation of the organism should be fluent and legible in the pattern of plan and the template of section. A building is not a machine; it does not work nor does it direct activity. However, there is a sense in which designs can be recognised as belonging to species, conforming to compositional categories and shaped around human routines. If a stair looks like it is in the wrong place in the plan, then something probably has to change to unify the order of the scheme. By a process of sustained sketching, modelling and overlay drawings, the expressive form of a scheme is whittled into existence.

Identity

There is an interesting interlude in the film *Notebook on Cities and Clothes* where Wim Wenders describes how he felt on his first encounter with some new clothes designed by Yohji Yamamoto:

> ...with this shirt and jacket it was different. From the beginning they were new and old at the same time. In the mirror I saw me of course, only better, more than me before and I had the strangest sensation I was wearing, yes I had no other words for it, I was wearing the shirt itself and the jacket itself and in them I was myself, I felt protected like a knight in his armour, by what, by a shirt and a jacket?

He explains the experience as an epiphany in which each particular garment emanates the essence of its kind – not merely another article of clothing but, enhancing his sense of identity, it takes on a more crucial, even archetypal status. It is not the comfort or the cut of the jacket that matters to Wenders, it is the personality of the piece that catches his imagination. In the following sequence in the film, Yamamoto slowly turns over the pages of a book of photographs, *Men in the Twentieth Century*, showing ordinary people in their working clothes, a book to which he returns in search of inspiration for his designs. He says he is affected by the faces of the figures as much as by the fabric of their costume, and he thinks about them while he is cutting and shaping the line of a dress. Fashion designer and film director are both captivated by the quest for character.

Time: Permanence, Continuity and the Living Present

When we say that we think of a building as a permanent thing, that is not to say it must stand intact for ever or that it cannot be changed. Working with existing buildings teaches us that a good building remains legible as a ruin, and that alterations and extensions can be incorporated as variations on the theme of the original form.

A building can be stripped back to its essentials, to reduce it to raw structure or spatial shell; overlaid with an intensification of its pattern, to change its scale or density; turned inside out, to make external spaces out of interior volumes; upside and down, to make gardens on the roof; and back to front, to give the middle of the block primacy over the edge condition. Radical transformations can occur within the life of a house, an institution or a town without compromise to its form and without damage to the idea of its permanence.

We do not think of buildings as ready solutions to immediate problems or expendable containers of short-term processes. Many buildings outlast their initial function and most buildings long outlive their original clients. Temporary constructions sometimes survive their projected redundancy to persist as fixed elements of their environment and, more mysteriously, certain structures endure beyond their physical destruction as lasting images in the collective memory.

We like to think of buildings as reservoirs of embedded energy. In some metaphysical sense, the spirit of an architect's endeavour dwells in the physical object of a building. The language of architecture is not written as in a poem or depicted as in a tapestry, yet intentions are embodied and ideas are communicated by buildings that speak to each other across the divide of time.

Once a plot of land becomes a building site, its potential is exchanged for another more committed condition of existence. In our fast-changing contemporary city, when a vacant or derelict site is developed, its melancholic languor is surrendered and uncounted possibilities are extinguished. Civic expectations have been eroded by cumulative breaches in urban continuity and only occasionally can a new construction be understood as a contribution to the public realm.

Instead of considering time as divided in linear chronological art-historical categories, with old buildings suspended in a petrified past and new buildings projected in a volatile future, we prefer to think of all buildings coexisting in the context of the living present. What is new today cannot remain new tomorrow. New buildings become assimilated and are eventually understood in relation to each other and to their place. Exclusive zones of heritage and development in city planning policies refrigerate history and disassociate contemporary activity from any cultural engagement with the slow deep background of the town.

The concept of permanence, whereby each project is considered as a vital element in the continuity and character of its context, is a radical one for architecture. It breaks down barriers between old and new, allows for creative reinterpretation of existing forms and facilitates a critical dialogue between established and emerging ideas. This is a principle that would favour evolution over restoration, intervention over preservation and form over style.

Application of such a strategy in practice requires knowledge of typology, historical research and intuitive analysis from first principles. To intervene in a courtyard the discipline of the type must be registered; to build on a street the system of the city needs to be evaluated. The perseverance to hold the line or the courage to change course is not the reaction of an individual moment but the exercise of an established craft.

Right
The Marco de Canavezes parish church designed by Alvaro Siza in Portugal. The height of the otherwise conventional doors stresses the liturgical procession from outside in.

Architecture Re-membered

Alvaro Siza's design for the parish church of Marco de Canavezes exemplifies a critical connection between tradition and creativity. The scheme is derived from the established form of a typical church with recognisable hierarchical elements of bell tower, baptismal font, narthex, nave, altar and apse each in their place and understood as essential to the meaning of the religious ritual. This is a lyrical work of extreme sophistication that combines the charm of childlike simplicity with a knowing command of precedent.

In a particularly interesting move, Siza slices and reverses the apse to redirect the focus of the ceremonial space. In the pre-Vatican 2 liturgy, the priest faced away from the people, or rather in the same direction as the people, and acted as a conductor of their concentration into the celestial dimension of the domelike structure or the arc of the apse. Understanding the liturgical about-face whereby the priest now looks to the congregation in a gathering space of worship, Siza re-members the traditional form, making the familiar seem strange, harnessing the established symbology in support of a new situation. Seamus Heaney has described one function of memory as a kind of disassembly and remaking of the past in which the parts of our history are dismembered in order to be remembered in a way that is useful to the present.

Metal-plated wooden doors stand on axis in conformity with convention, but being 10 metres high they are given an added dimension that emphasises the procession from outside in. A long slit window at standing eye-level undercuts the introversion of the sacred space and reminds us of the connections of the church with its parish community.

Much can be found in the architectural expression of Marco de Canavezes that makes homage to Le Corbusier's Romanesque rigour at La Tourette, leans on Loos, refers to Aalto's reserved space in the thickness of the walls of Vuoksenniska, and takes advantage of the space opened up in architecture by the virtuosity of Gehry. But the radical inspiration that locks the project into contact with its time and place is the subversive reworking of typology in the service of the meaning and significance of form.

Construction: Constructed Landscapes

The Icelandic landscape cannot properly be described as landscape in any strict definition of the term. Apart from its coastal conurbations, the island shows few signs of shaping by man. It is, on the contrary, overwhelmingly and spectacularly configured by nature. It is like a ground before time began, legible as evidence of the primal forces involved in the formation of the planet. Geography without history, it is a fresh and fragile terrain still in process, without fence or field, without definition of territory or place.

Icelanders believe the locus of origin of parliamentary democracy is situated at Pingvellir. The country's original population is said to have congregated annually on this site, a dramatic valley delineated by a geological fault on the one side and the crescent of a river meander on the other. A new form of societal governance was developed against an acoustic background of natural formation. Pingvellir can be described as being 'like an amphitheatre' and legend informs us that it was once used as such. But we need to know the story before we can interpret any sense of its former significance. History may have taken place in geography, but no place was made. No physical imprint remains to record the glory days of the founding of democracy or to act as evidence of the moment of cooperative endeavour.

In contrast, the Dutch landscape can only be understood as landscape in strictly definitional terms – land shaped by man, pure and simple. It is a hugely uncomplicated functional platform for production and consumption held in place by the most complex technological procedures. An even surface area, a superimposed cartography of canals and dykes, is formed by the same lines that are used to describe it on maps. A walker in this landscape has two points of reference, the ground underfoot and the distant horizon, vertical and horizontal coordinates in a two-dimensional environment. A train traveller in Holland navigates by the train timetable. In the absence of topographical landmarks such as valleys or mountains, distance is measured in time. History is defined without geography.

The Dutch farm represents a compelling example of the place-making instincts of an organised society. Clustered tightly in casually orthogonal relationships, the house and outbuildings hold their own against the open horizon. Outlined by trees and sheltered from the elements, these places make poignant enclosures for everyday life in an economic layout both emotional and practical in its internal arrangement. Viewed from the air, the self-contained settlements punctuate the nonhierarchical land-division system in a disconnected overlay. No boundaries emerge and no roads converge, the houses and land read like pins on a map, marking not making, like two separate ordinances independent and adrift from each other except for the phenomenon of their superimposed matrices. Habitation is comfortably accommodated and the land is efficiently cultivated, but neither builds into the other. The houses are not rooted to the site, and the field pattern does not bear the imprint of any physical engagement between building and landscape. Adjacent not interdependent, parallel not embedded, buildings are placed on the land like household crockery on a giant draining-board. No archaic resonance grounds the culture in place.

The traditional Chinese sunken court-cave houses, still functioning in Quian Ling, are an extreme expression of the merging of architecture and situation. These carved-out dwellings are like houses seen in reverse, organisms that have been turned inside out and made to eat themselves. Cell-like apartments present miniature elevations to the hollowed-out room of the central court. A variety of small spaces for sleeping and storage are burrowed behind the sheer surface of the excavated earth walls. The introverted roofless salon is the focus for communal life of the household. Thinking about these strange cavity constructions in sculptural terms suggests another kind of space making, the result of some imaginary casting process, a subtractive heaviness, solid space. Was this the sensation that Moretti recorded when he made plaster casts of the spatial volumes of Italian churches?

The cave dwellings (Sassi) in the Basilicata region of southern Italy fuel further reflections on the engagement of construction with context. From the 12th century, troglodytic inhabitants opportunistically occupied existing caves in the limestone escarpments. Byzantine refugees established the strategy, but the Sassi become architecturally interesting precisely at the point where the line is blurred between finding and making, between cave and construction. In the defining examples of the type throughout the derelict town of Matera, existing caverns have been further hollowed out to make interconnected chambers and hierarchically distinctive house plans. Material excavated from the interior has been used to build cut-stone threshold spaces, kitchens and chimneys. Stairways are half-

Walking through Matera demands a development of the language of our spatial experience in terms of landscape to building relationships. Simultaneously above and below, without and within, with a sometimes seamless continuity between geological formation and architectural form.

Reading the Site and Building Ground

The conceptual origins of some of our recent buildings have been derived directly from our understanding of the characteristics of their sites. We begin by thinking like archaeologists might do, metaphorically prodding the ground, searching for traces of what made it the way it is and sifting to unearth clues to inspire its further transformation. Our ambition is to build something completely new that feels like it was already there before we started, as if we had discovered the scheme rather than designed it.

Watching building sites proceed from excavation and foundation through the structural stages of frame and fabric to the finishing layers of skin and lining is a constant fascination of architectural practice. We are drawn to exploit the expressive potential that might be latent in the sequence of construction, seeking a tectonic clarity that neither mimics long-gone certainties of solid-wall technology nor acquiesces in the contemporary condition of interiors cut off from belonging to their outer shells.

We are looking for a way of thinking that could provide an integration between construction and site, a recasting of the redundant craft condition that by tradition would exploit local materials and harness indigenous skills. No valid vernacular pertains that can routinely as before produce a building born out of and belonging to its location. Given the proliferation of available technologies, the choice of construction becomes a serious matter, a cultural act that engineering or economics cannot be relied on to control. A critical issue for us as architects is the recognition of those conditions of the situation that could give significance to our choice of construction, embedding an initial sense of strategy that would remain evident in the eventual experience of the actual building. Δ

John Tuomey, a graduate of University College Dublin, worked with James Stirling in London and the Office of Public Works in Dublin prior to establishing O'Donnell + Tuomey in partnership with Sheila O'Donnell in 1988. He has taught at the Architectural Association, Cambridge University, Princeton, Harvard and Syracuse, and at Mendrisio in Switzerland. He was a winner (with Group 91) of the 2002 UIA Abercrombie Prize for Urban Design. O'Donnell + Tuomey is currently working on the design of cultural, social and educational projects in Ireland and the Netherlands.

carved, half-cantilevered out of the rock face. Internal walls of the caves have been pocketed with cupboards, and bed platforms remain as solid benches hewn out only to the point of functional necessity. The cave dwellings are clustered in close-knit social groupings, or *vicinati*, and the party walls between chambers have been quarried to minimal thicknesses with the economic precision of mineshaft technology.

Above
In the cave dwellings of Matera in the Basilicata region of Italy there is a seamless continuity between geological formation and architectural form.

Portugal has been isolated from Europe by both geography and language. With mountains along its border with Spain to the north and east and the Atlantic Ocean to the west, it is the westernmost outpost of continental Europe, and although Portuguese is a Romance language the spoken tongue is distant from the more familiar Spanish, French and Italian. As a consequence, Portugal historically looked out across the sea, where the navigational skills of its people enabled this small nation to build a worldwide empire with closer ties to South America, Africa and the Far East than to Europe.

Between 1928 and 1968, this isolation from its immediate neighbours was reinforced by the dictatorship of Dr Antonio de Oliveira Salazar. After Salazar, Portugal began to develop as a democracy. In 1986 the country elected its first civilian president for 60 years and also became a member of the European Community. A huge increase in foreign investment coupled with the massive influx of funding from the EC is now transforming Portugal's economy, which grew faster during the 1990s than most of its European neighbours.

The impact of this lively economy is clear. There are many projects under way to build transportation infrastructure and renew cities, to expand old universities and construct new ones. One of the consequences of the increased emphasis on higher education is that there are nearly seven times as many architects in Portugal today as in 1980.

In the 1998 monograph on his work, Alvaro Siza observes that this 'young generation of Portuguese architects is freer from inhibitions and contradictions (innovation or tradition, internationalism or regionalism) than earlier generations'. They are beginning their careers at a moment when Portugal is poised between the artisan-centred traditions of building that enriched the work of architects such as Siza, Tavora and Souto de Moura, and an increasingly industrialised construction culture.

The work of Manuel and Francisco Aires Mateus is emblematic of this new frame of mind. In addition to teaching at the Universidade Autonoma in Lisbon and at Mendrisio in Switzerland, they have completed a series of buildings in Portugal that are both attentive to their particular physical and cultural contexts and energetic in their exploration of territories of modernism.

Toll Booth

The completion in 2002 of the last segment of the major north–south autoroute in Portugal, which finally extends the highway south to the Algarve, is an important milestone in the modernisation of the country's road network. In recognition of its significance, the design of the toll booth for the new road was given special consideration through an invited design competition won by Aires Mateus. While these architects have constructed buildings of varying sizes in the context of village, campus and city, this is their first venture into the territory of infrastructure.

The scheme seeks to strike a balance between stasis and motion – that is, between the toll booth as a gateway and the continuity of the road. The gateway is defined by a series of white concrete canopies that shelter the toll booths. The booths sit on raised islands of black concrete that blend imperceptibly with the asphalt surface of the road. In contrast with the regular spacing of the booths, which is determined by the width of the vehicular lanes, the overlapping canopies vary in height and breadth. Each is an inverted pyramid supported on a single central column. Cast on site, these concrete canopies, conceived as a grove of 'trees', create a constructed landscape that marks the threshold to the Algarve.

In contrast with the canopies, which are silhouetted against the sky, the staff offices and support facilities for the toll station are organised in a single-storey building tucked into the slope of the rising ground alongside the highway. This excavated space is covered by a planted roof designed to read as an extension of the ground. The only part of the building that is visible is its fully glazed facade which faces the road. Emphasising the directional and linear character of the highway, the 160-metre long facade extends far beyond the limits of the actual building. Where there is accommodation behind, walls perpendicular to the facade are held back and connected by glazed fins. When the building ends, the glazed wall that continues is spaced 600 millimetres in front of the concrete retaining wall.

By day, the canopies create a visual barrier across the highway that is defined by shadow. At night, the soffits of the canopies are washed with light from lamps concealed in the roofs of the toll booths, creating an equally clear visual barrier of light. In contrast, lights set in the floor between the retaining wall and glazed facade of the support building create a line of light embedded in the ground, emphasising the continuity of movement on either side of the barrier. In this scheme, distinctions between constructed and excavated space, and between containment and release that inform the buildings of Aires Mateus are played out compellingly at the larger scale of infrastructure and landscape.

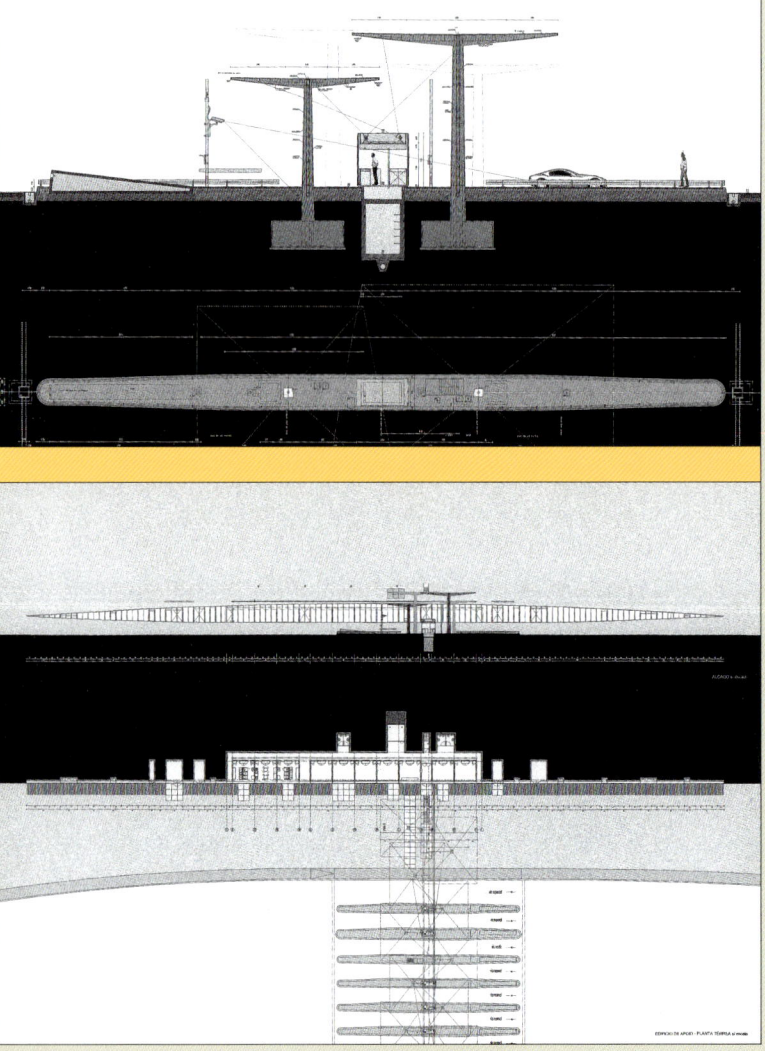

Toll Booth, Algarve, Portugal, 2002

Opposite
Plans and sections show the 'avenue' of concrete trees that provides shade at the toll booths and the offices cut into the slope of the embankment.

House in Alenquer

Old and new are brought into sharp focus in this scheme for a 100-square-metre weekend house in Alenquer, 30 kilometres northeast of Lisbon. Embedded in the dense urban fabric of a medieval hillside town, the site was occupied by the ruins of a house and barn. The work required to reinstate the original buildings was extensive and proved too costly. Instead, architects Manuel and Francisco Aires Mateus have simply stabilised, rerendered and painted the existing walls.

Working within the ruins of the previous house, they have designed a freestanding dwelling and excavated a pool within the former enclosure of the barn. In contrast with the existing walls, which follow the medieval contours of the village, this new house is rationally ordered. A series of small orthogonal volumes projects from the simple two-storey rectangular body of the building, creating an intricate sequence of spaces that are ambiguously both inside and outside, and which charge the void between old and new.

Approaching the house along a narrow lane, a large gated opening in the old wall provides an enclosed on-site parking place. Pedestrians enter down a few steps in a narrow gap between the retained wall fragments into a court between house and pool that spills out onto a planted terrace overlooking the village. The living/dining space and open kitchen occupy the slightly raised ground floor of the house, with three bedrooms and two bathrooms above.

Although economical in area, the house is spatially complex. At the top of the skylit stair, one bedroom is reached via a galvanised grated bridge, and the master bedroom and each bathroom open into walled outdoor courts. In places, the void between old and new makes double-height walled courts open to the sky, and in others single-storey outdoor rooms shaded and sheltered by the cantilevered volumes above. The walled courts on the second floor of the house allow the void to penetrate the body of the house and to be occupied at the upper level.

The new construction comes tantalisingly close to but does not touch the old walls. Like the lens of a camera, the ends of the cantilevered volumes are fully glazed, framing uncomposed collages of ground and sky and glimpses of the village through unglazed openings in the retained walls.

The open-endedness of the projecting volumes creates an illusion of generosity within the constraints of an extremely compact plan.

The slippage, or lack of alignment, between old and new openings maintains the integrity of each construction and creates a range of depths in the field of vision.

With both the walls and the house painted white, obvious material distinctions between old and new are avoided yet the inherent nature of each construction remains clear. The original house and barn were made of masonry walls with timber floors and roofs. Only the masonry survived the ravages of time so that the spaces now contained by the walls are open to the sky. Because of the demands of their load-bearing construction, these walls rest solidly on the ground and are pierced only by small, narrow openings. The new house, which is made of reinforced site-cast concrete, follows a different logic that is able to make open-ended tubes of space that extend laterally, seemingly without support. These distinctions in the making of old and new augment the rich spatial relationships, which are in turn animated by the play of light and shadow in this modest house.

House in Alenquer, Portugal, 2001
The new house in the village of Alenquer has been built within the walls of a former house and barn to create outdoor spaces between, and frame views of, the landscape beyond.

Opposite
Sections.

Right, top
Ground floor plan.

Right, bottom
First floor plan.

Universidade Nova Rectory

The imposing facade of a former Jesuit school dominates this large and prominent site adjacent to one of the main freeways into Lisbon. When it was built, the school looked out over farmland from its position at the edge of a plateau. Now absorbed into the city, the old building is surrounded by new office towers and housing. The former school and its remaining land form the core of the Universidade Nova in Lisbon.

The rectory provides offices for the university administration together with honorific public spaces that are used for convocations, ceremonies and cultural events. It is intended to be the catalyst of a new order that makes sense of this residual site. Together with the former school, the massing of the rectory generates a new public square of imposing scale. The administrative offices are housed in an eight-storey tower that forms the backdrop to this square and a monumental flight of steps that defines the entrance to this hillside extension to the university precinct. Taking advantage of the sloping site, the public foyers and auditoriums are tucked under the podium formed by the square and steps. It is hoped that the university will reinforce this well-considered move as it proceeds with the development of both buildings and landscape on the larger site.

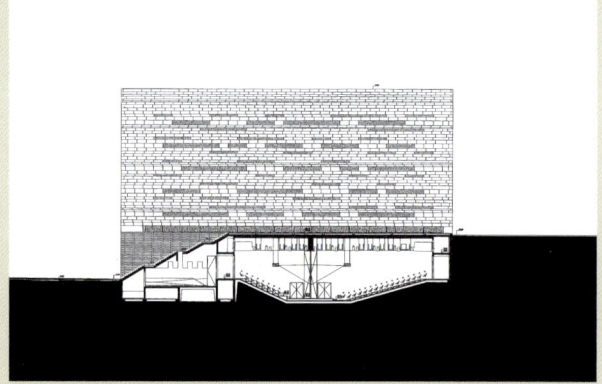

The rectory is entered from the north at the foot of the monumental stair. The entrance foyer, which extends the length of the building, is the hinge between the public spaces in the podium and a full-height void along the east face of the office tower. Although the tall, slender entrance facade has a clear vertical thrust externally, the emphasis switches immediately inside the door where the sense of compression and horizontal extension is augmented by the understanding that the foyers are conceived as a void between apparently thick roof and ground slabs. The long and generously wide entrance hall is a single-storey space with daylight admitted only through the glazed facades at the narrow ends of the tower. In contrast to the bright sunlight outside, this provides a transition to the foyers that, although finished predominantly with white-painted plaster, are pleasantly cool and dark.

A large flat-floor lecture room and a raked auditorium, which can be used either as a single space or divided to create two assembly rooms, are conceived as islands that are pulled away from the boundary walls of the podium and surrounded by circulation space. Support functions such as cloakrooms are also articulated as smaller islands within the void.

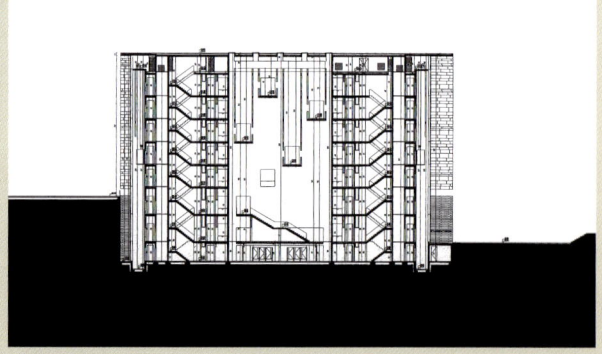

Universidade Nova Rectory, Lisbon, 2002

Top to bottom
Site plan.
Section through auditorium.
Section through auditorium and offices.
Section through offices.

Thickness above is revealed by long slender skylights carved into the poche of the roof, and below by the excavation of stairs and ramps into the thickness of the floor. The rooflights combine concealed artificial lighting along their length with indirect daylight at their ends. Placed precisely under the skylights, the stairs and ramps cut into the wood-strip floor are lined entirely with richly veined white marble.

The office tower is efficiently planned with services and cores concentrated in a three-metre-wide band along the east face of the building, and all offices facing west overlooking the terrace and monumental steps. Moving from the entrance hall to the open stair that serves the two floors of offices at the base of the building, the compression within the podium is emphatically released into a full-height void. Like the foyers, this void is occupied by islands of accommodation. Serving the offices, these waiting areas are compact in plan and generous in section. While it would have been easy to span the three metres between corridor and external wall, the volumes are suspended to isolate the waiting rooms from the adjacent walls in order to reiterate the relationship between solid and void that is played out in the podium below.

Within the building, all openings are faced with marble. The detail is elegant in its simplicity, with the marble lining cut to a 45-degree bevel and used as the plaster stop, producing a razor-sharp flush joint at the corner and concealing the thickness – or thinness – of each material. It is a detail that is refined yet also ordinary in a building culture in which stone is ubiquitous and wet instead of one where dry trades predominate. In contrast with this interior detailing, which is rooted in traditional construction techniques, the exterior envelope is an open-jointed stone rain-screen that is detailed to wrap over the roof to clad the long facades of the building. While this flush stone wrapper has no openings on the east facade, it is perforated by randomly disposed horizontal slots of recessed windows on the west elevation. Each cellular office consequently has a unique combination of openings at floor, eye and high level.

This strategy conceals the precise reading of the floor levels, monumentalising the building as a backdrop to the square and steps. In contrast with the interior detailing, where the stone creates the illusion that the entire wall is of stone, the exterior envelope reads clearly as a thin skin. Although the stone does come out of the ground on the east facade where the base of the building is articulated by thin 'compressed' coursing, its nonload-bearing character is made clear on the west face where it hovers above the new ground of the stone podium, isolated by a continuous slot of glazing.

The rectory rehabilitates the former Jesuit school by returning it to a position of prominence and making it an active participant in the creation of a new civic space for the university. The formal simplicity and rational planning of the rectory are excellent foils for its spatial complexity. The exploration of excavated and constructed space and of the representation of this space by thick and thin systems of construction is a consistent consideration in the work of Aires Mateus. *Δ* AWL

Universidade Nova Rectory, Lisbon, 2002

The auditorium and foyers are planned underground to create a monumental flight of steps leading to the campus while the offices form a tall stone wall at the boundary.

Styria, the second largest of the nine Austrian *Länder*, lies on the southern side of the Alps. The impact of this Alpine barrier, combined with long histories of immigration and invasion, located it as the eastern frontier of the Holy Roman Empire. These conditions have continued to define it as a distinct territory.

In the early 19th century the modernisation of the region was encouraged by the energetic Archduke Johann and the population of the Land of Styria increased by almost 50 per cent between 1849 and 1914.

Although Vienna is only 150 kilometres away from Graz, Austria's second largest city and the capital of Styria, it is a long journey along winding roads and train tracks that extend through an intricate network of tunnels. Situated at the edge this is an area of considerable natural beauty yet also a thriving industrial region. A place open to experiment, Styria, free of the burdens of tradition that predominate in Vienna, looks to the south beyond the confines of Austria and connects directly to Italy and the Balkans.

Ernst Giselbrecht

Conference Centre at Seggau Castle

Since 1954 this 'town on the hill' has been under the direction of prelate Karl Wagner. Working from the castle, at the centre of an estate of approximately 800 hectares, he has sought to balance the institution's social obligations with a plan to allow for the careful restoration and sensitive use of the historic buildings. The castle is extensive and it was proposed to retain a part for the residence of the bishop and to create a new residential conference centre in the remaining space.

The first stage of this new programme of work, designed by the architect Konrad Frey, included the restoration and redecoration of existing spaces in the existing south wing and the construction of a congress hall alongside. Completed in 1993 it prompted a plan for further development that could combine the restoration of other spaces in the existing buildings with the addition of new buildings. This strategy allowed for the addition of the most up-to-date facilities

and the formulation of a new identity for a conference centre contained within the historic core of the castle.

The master plan for the subsequent phases, prepared by architect Ernst Giselbrecht, was initiated at the end of 1996. Working in close consultation with the bishop, the community and the government officials responsible for the planning and restoration of historic buildings, Giselbrecht developed detailed proposals that located the conference centre within an existing range of the castle buildings linked to a slither of new building.

Designed to connect with the recently constructed congress hall the new building defines the outer southern edge of the development. While a part of the slither was to sit alongside the existing buildings, another part of it would project into a second courtyard bounded by a freestanding stable block to define a new conference garden. In addition the redevelopment of a strip of basement space alongside the existing building on the western boundary would not only provide much-needed storage space but also create a new entrance onto a rooftop terrace overlooking a new open-air pool set within the landscape of the garden.

Conference Centre at Seggau Castle, Styria, 2002

Opposite
The restored buildings of the old castle which are connected to the spaces in the new conference court.

Above
The glassy wall of the new conference centre defines one edge of the residential courtyard, which has a large pool.

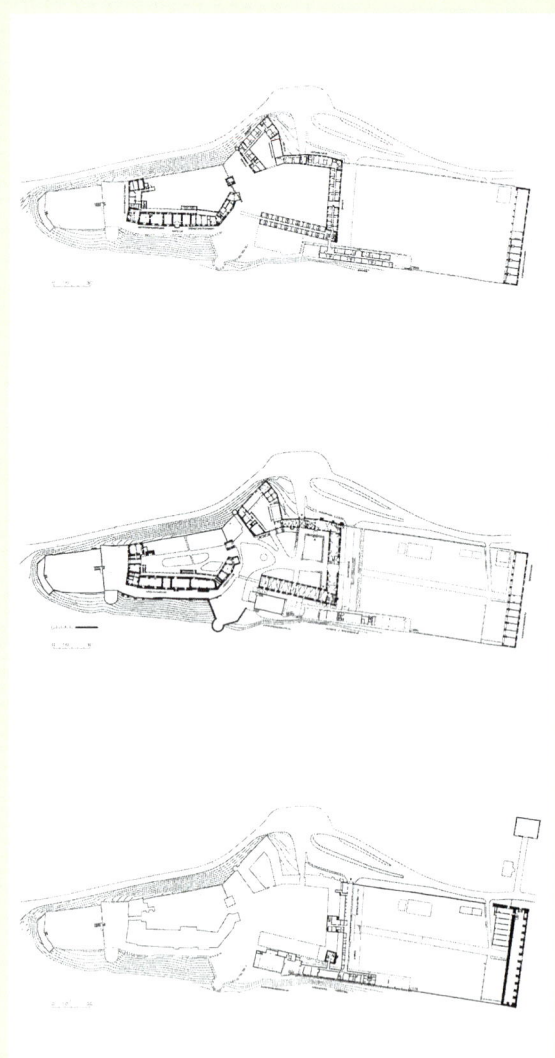

In an attempt to
distinguish between
new and old and
at the same time
create a focus for
the conference centre,
the new buildings
at Seggau provide
a conspicuous
contrast with their
historic neighbours.

Conference Centre at Seggau Castle, Styria, 2002

Opposite, left
Upper level plan.
Ground floor plan.
Basement plan.

Opposite, right
A stair from the upper floor connects into the new courtyard garden and marks the edge of the walled compound.

Above
The double-skin thermal glass wall of the conference centre reflects the colonnaded facade of the restored stable block at the edge of the garden.

In an attempt to distinguish between new and old and at the same time create a focus for the conference centre, the new buildings at Seggau provide a conspicuous contrast with their historic neighbours. Circulation spaces – important places in a conference centre where visitors can orientate themselves and also meet colleagues informally – are clearly expressed as light, open walkways of glass and steel. Both hallways and staircases are attenuated to define the edge of the new conference garden and through their extension become part of the landscape. They also emphasise the walls of the castle enclosure.

The public spaces are planned on three levels in a series of open glassy rooms with views to the garden. The residential rooms, planned along a double-loaded corridor, are organised so that the long dimension of the room is on the external wall and provides generous views over the garden and to the horizon beyond.

For these new buildings, Giselbrecht has added wood to his palette of steel and glass. Fixed in modular panels, the rich oxblood varnished cladding reads effectively as a new and conspicuous layer introduced against the stone garden walls, greenery and restored masonry of the existing buildings. This idea of layering is also expressed in the detail of the long glassy elevation of the new building. Trained both as a mechanical engineer and an architect, Giselbrecht has here underlined his interest in design and building performance. To screen the rooms on this exposed facade, a composite wall of layered glass that effectively combines reflections of buildings and landscape is also detailed to be ventilated. This double-glass wall acts like the fly sheet on a tent and protects the rooms from cold winds in winter and the heat of the sun during summer months.

The new conference centre is almost hidden. Tucked discreetly into the fabric of the historic castle at Seggau it is a scheme which, once discovered, works successfully at many levels. The buildings are clearly different from their neighbours yet effectively integrated within the castle. With sensitive siting and the thoughtful use of new materials selected and detailed to address environmental concerns, this design for the Seggau Castle Conference Centre creates a place for meditation and an inspiring mountain retreat. ∆ BC

Confounding Lightness

Stone is one of the most ecologically sensitive materials and performs well. A series of new stone buildings in the south of France highlights one architect's attempt to connect design and material research.

Gilles Perraudin

Architect and engineer Gilles Perraudin has aggressively explored the potential of materials through practice. Working in an office within a walled garden on the outskirts of Lyon and far from the bustle and frenzy of Paris, he and his former partner Francoise-Helene Jourda designed a series of significant buildings. All developed innovative ideas about the use of materials and their environmental impact.

One of their first projects, a housing scheme in Isle d'Abeau, was built using rammed earth, a material traditionally used in the region. And in their competition-winning designs for a new architecture school in Lyon, and a later scheme for the academy at Herne-Sodingen, the architects advanced other ideas to design dynamic glass envelopes combined with heavy timber structural frames and specially developed steel castings. Detailed to respond to differing uses and varying climates, these were schemes that were also endorsed through collaborative programmes of research on performance and supported by European Community grants.

Since 1998, Perraudin has been working in the south of France and exploring the potential of one particular material. Stone, he argues, is one of the most ecologically sensitive materials available. With no energy required in its transformation, it performs well structurally, thermally and acoustically, requires virtually no maintenance and almost invariably ages gracefully. In an attempt to exploit these qualities, Perraudin has been working on the design of new buildings in which load-bearing walls are constructed from large cut-stones. Using limestone from a quarry in the village of Vers-Pont-du-Gard, between Nimes and Avignon, the stone is cut in blocks that are

approximately 1 metre high by 2.25 metres long, and between 52 and 65 centimetres thick.

Perraudin's construction system is extremely simple. Once extracted from the quarry by direct sawing, the stone is delivered to site by truck where it can be immediately craned from the truck bed and placed into position in a standard bonded wall construction. The site operation is quick, dry and without waste. The mass of this heavy envelope performs well environmentally, and by planning openings that conform to the module of the cut block it is a system that obviates the need for additional lintels.

Wine Cellar, Vauvert

In 1998, Perraudin initiated a project specifically to test the material and this way of building. The wine cellar at Vauvert in the Camargue is a 900-square-metre single-storey building that provides space for storage together with offices and a reception area. The compact plan has been organised around a single open courtyard and the new building enclosure consists of load-bearing bonded blocks of limestone.

Each of these blocks is 1.05 metres by 2.6 metres by 52 centimetres thick and weighs 2.5 tons. Openings are kept to a minimum, and in this Mediterranean climate where the extreme differences in temperature can create problems for the proper storage of wine, the building has performed well. The cost of the material is offset by the speed of construction – the building was built in 30 days – and the simplicity of the design of the archaic masonry structure. It is a design informed by a deep understanding of the properties of the material and of construction techniques perfected in vernacular buildings.

Winery at Vauvert, 1998

Wine Cellar, Nizas

A second wine cellar, designed for a site at Nizas and consisting of two buildings linked by a shaded courtyard, used the same stone cut in blocks of the same size. However, while the materials were the same, the form and shape of the envelope and the openings that were formed in it were substantially different from the earlier project at Vauvert.

Apprentice Training Centre

In subsequent projects, Perraudin has been able to test the potential of stone in other ways. His competition-winning scheme for the new Apprentice Training Centre at Nimes Marguerittes, completed in 1999, proposed a group of single-storey buildings organised around a sequence of open landscaped courtyards. The buildings in this 4600-square-metre complex, designed not to exceed the height of the existing olive trees on the site, have also been planned to house a range of different uses. The stone pavilions accommodate workshops, classrooms, restaurants, lecture theatres and offices, but all have been built using the same constructional system of large load-bearing blocks of stone.

Perraudin is not only preoccupied with the use of this singular material but also with developing ways of applying the latest construction technology to natural stone instead of reverting to romanticised notions of handicraft. In all of his projects, the stone is cut with great precision using sophisticated equipment, and work on site is highly mechanised to ensure both speed and accuracy. On the basis of his studies and built work in the region, Perraudin has found that the solidity, strength, appearance and performance of stone make it a viable and welcome alternative to the widespread infatuation with lightness and transparency. In order to advance his research, Gilles Perraudin teaches as a professor of architecture at L'École d'Architecture du Languedoc-Roussillon and is also actively involved at L'École d'Architecture de Grenoble – an institution that has a well-established and respected research programme into the use of earth and stone in architecture.

Although building in stone seems quite appropriate in the context of the historic cities of southern France, many new buildings there – as in other parts of the world – are constructed using materials that are synthetic, mass-produced and globally distributed. In this context, Gilles Perraudin's use of load-bearing stone is clearly radical and at the boundaries of contemporary architectural practice. ⌂ BC

One of the most urban nations in the world, Canada has
to deal with all the cultural, social and economic issues
that entails. Its French-Anglo heritage has given it its
own specific cultural blend, as explored by 'Laboratoires'
(pp 80–84) The vast scale and emptiness of the natural
landscape still renders even a metropolis like Vancouver, as
discussed by Patkau Architects (pp 75–79) relatively isolated
in global terms. And two recently completed projects by Shim-
Sutcliffe clearly demonstrate how extreme climatic conditions
can influence the design of buildings.

Shim-Sutcliffe

Moorelands Camp

Moorelands Camp is a residential centre for summer educational and recreational programmes. Run by a nonprofit charity, the programmes are for disadvantaged children who live in Toronto, and provide opportunities for those children to spend time in the country during the summer months. The camp is located on a remote site in the Haliburton Highlands in Ontario, north of Toronto. Here the Canadian Shield – granite bedrock exposed after the last ice age – shapes a landscape that is made up of many small lakes surrounded by dense forests. Situated on a peninsula on Lake Kawagama, the only access to the camp is by boat.

The invitation to design a new dining hall provided an opportunity to develop a scheme that embodied both the spirit of the camp and its site. The project was equivalent to building a large barn yet because of the difficulties of access and transportation of materials, this was a building that had to be built with small sticks. Using the smallest size members possible – two by fours – the architects sought to develop a scheme that would create the largest space and the longest possible spans. By combining these sticks with light steel elements, the potential of

small-scale dimensioned lumber was exploited to create a 36-foot-wide column-free space.

Many buildings at older summer camps were constructed of logs and as a result are heavy and dark. Stark contrasts result from having natural light primarily at the perimeter. In an attempt to invert this norm, Shim-Sutcliffe wanted to make a space that had natural light at the centre. Because the building was used throughout the day, there was an interest in designing a hall that would define a distinct place in the woods and a focus for the camp. Using a standard industrial motorised greenhouse glazing system, they created a central rooflight that introduced daylight and incorporated natural ventilation. Integrated with 12 glue-laminated trusses, this formed a structural 'lantern' through the middle of the space. As a result, the large room – 36 feet wide and 100 feet long – not only has sunlight at the centre of the space during the day but also glows like a lantern at night.

The hall has been designed with a covered porch and a ramped series of terraces at one end. Together these form sheltered outdoor areas that are directly connected to the lake and the wooded landscape beyond and can be used for camp activities and informal meetings.

While the camp is intensively used by groups of children throughout the summer months, it is not used during the remainder of the year. During this time, because of the severe weather and the need to provide security, the dining hall has to be closed down. However, rather than assuming that this would happen

Moorelands Camp dining hall, Haliburton Highlands, Ontario, 2000

in an ad hoc fashion using whatever materials might be at hand, the external wall of the hall is designed with a series of adjustable folding screens. These are opened during the summer and provide generous views out to the surrounding landscape. They also help to encourage natural ventilation and provide shading from the summer sun while defining an intimately scaled walkway around the perimeter of the building. At the end of the summer season they are folded down and secured to protect the building through the winter.

Although the building was competitively tendered and awarded to the lowest bidder, it became obvious after a short time on site that the appointed contractor was having difficulties doing the job. As a result the architects contacted Brian Mackay-Lyons, an architect colleague in Nova Scotia who had also designed and built a series of buildings on remote sites. Mackay-Lyons gathered together a crew of carpenters who then travelled to Ontario. Once at Lake Kawagama they camped on the site and completed the construction of the building in readiness for the coming summer season. It was, as one of the team said, 'just like building a boat'.

In its form, materials and the manner of its construction the design of the dining hall seeks to connect this large new room, the functional and spiritual centre of the camp, with the spectacular natural landscape. And at the same time it embodies the generous spirit and shared ideals of both the client and the camp community.

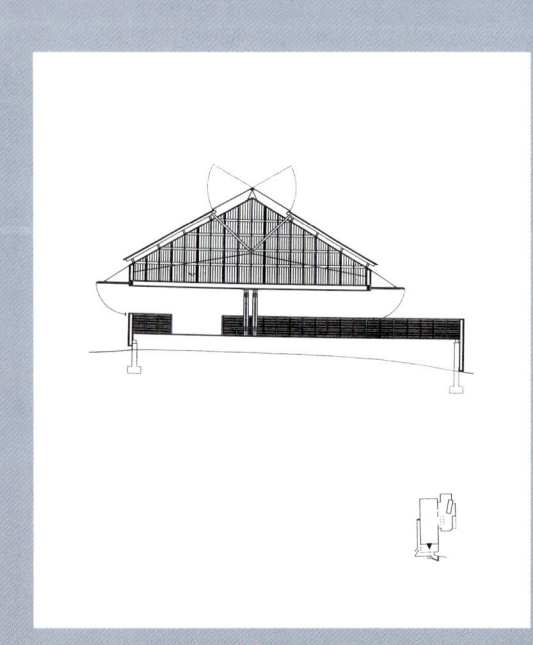

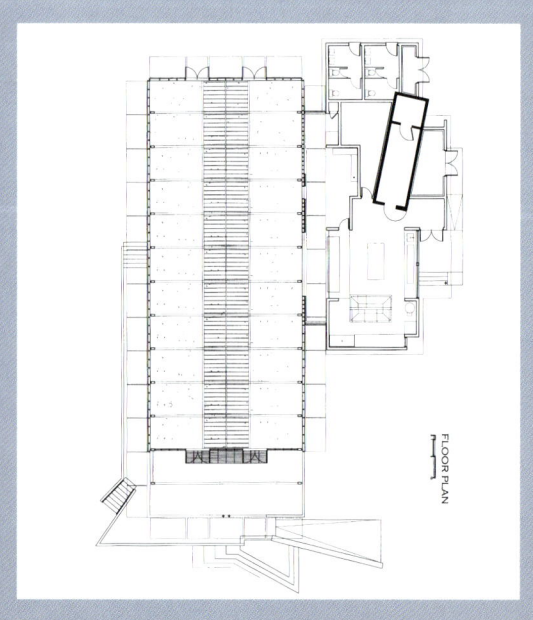

Moorelands Camp dining hall, Haliburton Highlands, Ontario, 2000

Right
Sectional elevation.

Far right
Ground-floor plan.

Boathouse in Muskoka

A new Boathouse in Muskoka, built after the dining hall at Moorelands Camp, is also situated in an isolated and rugged setting. Located on a remote island in Lake Muskoka in northern Ontario, the building consists of two indoor boat slips and an additional outdoor mooring on the water with a sleeping cabin above. Here the architects sought to develop a design that benefited from traditional local patterns of building in wood and also of constructing buildings over the water.

Like the Adirondack camps of upstate New York, this boathouse has been considered as a 'hut', albeit a sophisticated one, located in the wilderness. However, it also seeks to advance the simultaneous invention of new ways to posit a modernist tradition. This approach was inspired by the design of long cruising boats constructed of mahogany, and built in the area. Consequently the project sought to find a balance not only between building and nature, but one informed by the vernacular and 20th-century Modernism.

For everything that is constructed above the water on these lakes, there is an infrastructure that is hidden under water. Traditionally, builders

in this area first construct a series of heavy timber cribs that form the foundations for a building on the water. To do this, they wait until the middle of winter when the lake is frozen over and then draw out a plan on the ice that defines the extent of the building and the detailed location of the cribs that will eventually support it. Based on this plan, and using chain saws, they cut holes in the ice where the cribs will be located. Sleepers are then placed over the holes and the cribs are built up over the sleepers on the ice. Having measured the depth of the water and the slope of the bottom of the lake with sticks and tapes, the crib structures are constructed to precise dimensions using large squared sections of hemlock. Once they are completed, the sleepers are cut and the structures are allowed to sink into the water. The cribs are filled with granite boulders and provide an underwater substructure for the wooden superstructure of the boathouse above. This system of construction has been used for many years and enables the builder to work during the winter. It also ensures that the construction starts from a pure plane of ice – a way of building that is considerably easier than trying to build foundations from boats!

The design of the boathouse was inspired by the notion of creating a hut with a heavy overcoat. Heavy timbers, rescued from a demolished warehouse in

Boathouse, Muskoka, 1999

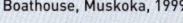

Kitchener-Waterloo, were remilled and refitted to make an outer skin. It is as if the underwater infrastructure of the cribs has been pulled up out of the water and made visible. In this way, something that is normally suppressed becomes an important part of the architecture. A second structure, more like the refined construction of a wooden boat, has been built within the heavy outer layer. A series of habitable spaces is formed between and within the two layers of construction. The stairs and outdoor porches are planned in the spaces between the layers. To further underline the distinction between the parts of the building, the indoor boat slips are lined with birch plywood while the habitable rooms in the sleeping cabin above are finished in Douglas fir and mahogany and detailed like the spaces of a yacht.

Prompted by the client, the architects developed a series of special fittings for this project. One, a boat cleat, was designed to avoid stubbing toes on the dock. The cleat combines a specially designed housing made from a custom bronze casting with a ready-made stainless-steel shackle purchased from a marine supplier. This made it possible for the cleat to be installed

flush with the dock. In addition, Shim-Sutcliffe designed custom door handles and light fixtures. A screen-door pull, made from red-bronze rods, alludes to a snow shoe while light fittings designed to go under soffits combine a refrigerator light bulb – made to take account of temperature differential fluctuations – with a bronze housing that acts as a sconce. For another hanging light in the covered outdoor porches they used the largest Mason jar, made for preserving fruits and vegetables. Elliptical planes coated with a phosphorescent paint normally used by fishermen are suspended within a specially designed housing of stainless steel and copper, giving the impression of moths fluttering around a light bulb. These experiments enabled the architects not only to explore the potential of everyday found objects but also to speculate about their transformation by adding custom pieces to create a new object.

Although these two buildings were designed for clients with quite different requirements and budgets, the demands of building in remote settings influenced the way that both were designed. Both make use of local knowledge and skills, explored the potential of familiar materials and sought to benefit from the problems of making architecture in the Canadian wilderness. BC

Boathouse, Muskoka, 1999

Right
The interior spaces of the sleeping cabin have been detailed to emphasise the layering of the building skin.

Far right, top
Dock-level plan.

Far right, bottom
Cabin-level plan.

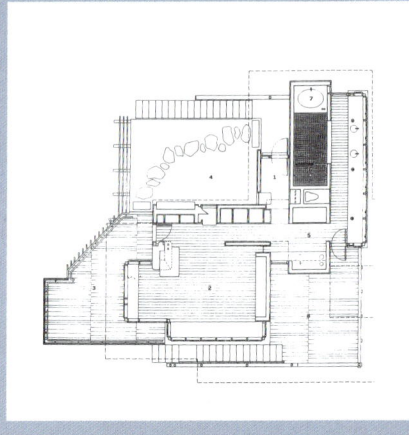

Other Realms of Invention:

John Patkau of Patkau Architects in Conversation with Brian Carter

Patkau Architects was founded in 1978, and since 1984 its studio has been located in western Canada, an area that is geographically remote in global terms. It is, however, a situation that the architects have turned to their advantage; with few opportunities to refer to international consultants, they have had to rely on resourcefulness and invention.

We know that practising in Vancouver inevitably means that a substantial amount of our work will be elsewhere. In the past few years this has not only taken us to islands off the coast of the Pacific Northwest but has also provided opportunities for our office to work on the design of large new buildings in Montreal and Philadelphia. In this context, any discussion of remoteness or being at the edge tends to focus more on our own location than on that of the work.

For example, the recently completed Agosta House that we designed was for a couple who moved from Manhattan to Washington State and wanted a house where they could live while continuing their professional work and cultivating a garden. It is located on a small and predominantly rural island off the Pacific coast on a 43-acre site that is largely covered by a second-growth Douglas fir forest. Almost a quarter of the site is dedicated to a perpetual conservation easement, and while it is partially contained by the forest, views out to the northwest are over rolling fields and across the Haro Strait to the Gulf Islands of British Columbia and the horizon beyond.

Ironically, however, we do not see this as a remote site. Certainly it is off the mainland and a ferry ride away, but Friday Harbour, the main town on the island, is still a place with capable local builders, a reasonable range of materials and good concrete suppliers. FedEx goes there –

and that certainly contradicts any ideas of remoteness! We find that in working at this domestic scale and benefiting from the resourcefulness of local house builders, almost anything is possible.

In a setting like this, it is the natural landscape rather than the constraints of building in an only apparently remote place that provides us with inspiration. At the Agosta House this translates into a scheme that is stretched across the meadow. Like a dam, it divides the site to form an enclosed space on the southeast. It is as if that space is then released through the house to the panorama below – a sea of picturesque fields and waterways. In response to this idea and to the slope of the site, the section of the building has been 'battered'. The spatial organisation of the house is the result of extruding this simple section and then manipulating it by erosion or insertion. In this way, a relatively small building is transformed into an element that reads at the vast scale of the landscape.

If you look carefully at the drawings of the Agosta House, you can trace a history. Not only is the plan drawn out to make this a defining wall of building that creates distinct areas on the site, but it also captures outdoor spaces in ways that recall our design for Strawberry Vale School. We consider that building is a milestone in the development of our practice. Designed in 1992, it also forms a boundary – between a forest of Garry oaks and Victoria's suburban fringe – and has a 'sidedness' that can be detected in the development of the Agosta House. The design of Strawberry Vale School

Top
Agosta House, Washington State, 2000

Bottom, left and right
Strawberry Vale School, Victoria, Vancouver Island, 1996

was a struggle for us; the fragmentary forms were hard to invent. However, while the building is obviously larger than a house, we attempted to take the values of a house and turn them into a school. We were also able to build it using residential construction techniques.

The form of the classrooms, the way they make outdoor teaching spaces and the fracturing of the section to scoop in daylight were all influential in the design of the Agosta House. Yet in contrast to the embodied energy of the school the house seeks out a sense of calmness. This calmness has come as a result of our renewed interest in simplicity and the seemingly endless

flexibility that rationalised construction systems offer. By making use of that flexibility, we can limit complexity in our projects rather than seeking to expand it. The construction industry has got our attention!

Currently, we are working on the design and construction of the new Gleneagles Community Centre – a building of moderate size like the school. This centre will provide a range of different facilities for people living in West Vancouver, including art rooms, a youth centre, childcare and counselling, a café with a community 'living room' and a large gymnasium. The form of the building is a simple extrusion – we have come to understand that it is important to seek out the most direct ways of constructing things. In this project, we are using large

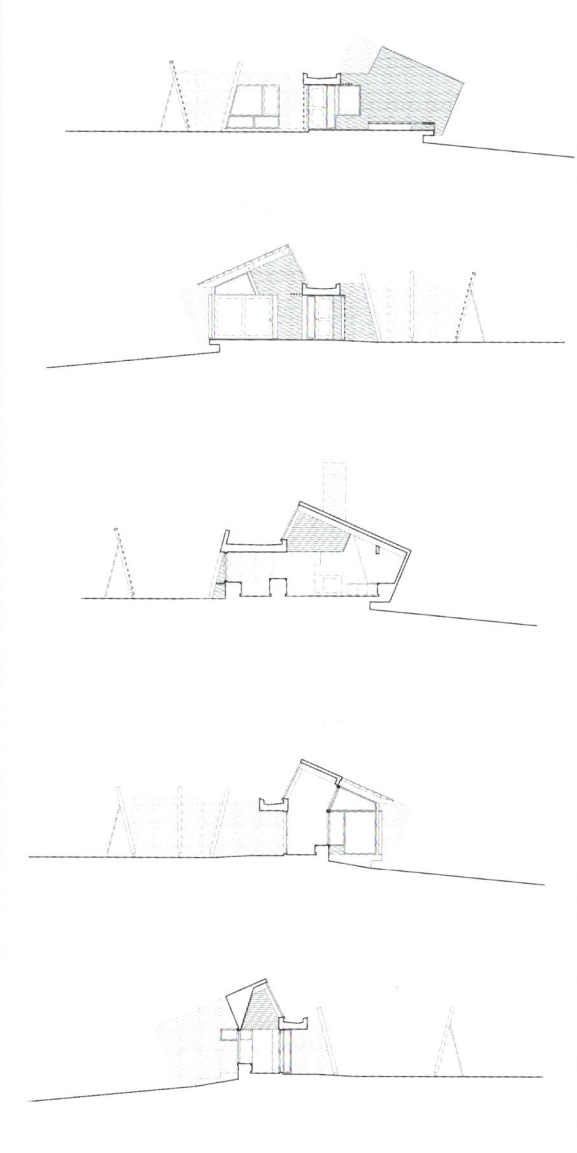

amounts of reinforced concrete with an oversailing parasol roof constructed of heavy timber. The design of the centre, and in particular that of the gymnasium, led us to look to the construction industry again for inspiration. The tall end-walls of the gymnasium are tilt-up concrete panels. This is a tried and tested construction system that gives you a phenomenal wall for your dollar!

But we also wanted to capitalise on the mass of material in these walls and have consequently designed them so that they are used for radiant heating and cooling. The thermal energy needed to supply this system is provided by water-to-water heat pumps via a ground source heat exchanger. In this way these concrete walls become a performative skin. This is a development from the more expressive forms

that we have explored in other projects and reflects our continuing interest in performance and the integration of the various systems of the building.

Our remoteness in Vancouver can make this pursuit a difficult one. We rarely have the resources to bring in specialist consultants to work with us, however being remote can also be a benefit because it encourages us to be inventive. On this project, we have discovered an excellent group of people locally and this has made the design process all the more rewarding. The composition and commitment of the team are important too because design integration creates interdependencies. It is critical that those interdependencies are understood and that there is mutual trust if that integration is to work.

These aspects of invention in design have been influential in the design of La Grande Bibliothèque du Québec. This is a project that presents other orders of

Agosta House, Washington State, 2000

Top left
Site plan.

Right
Cross sections.

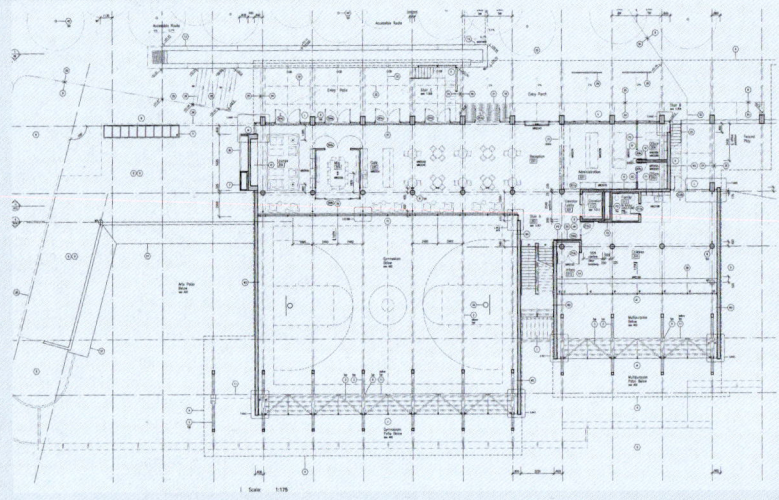

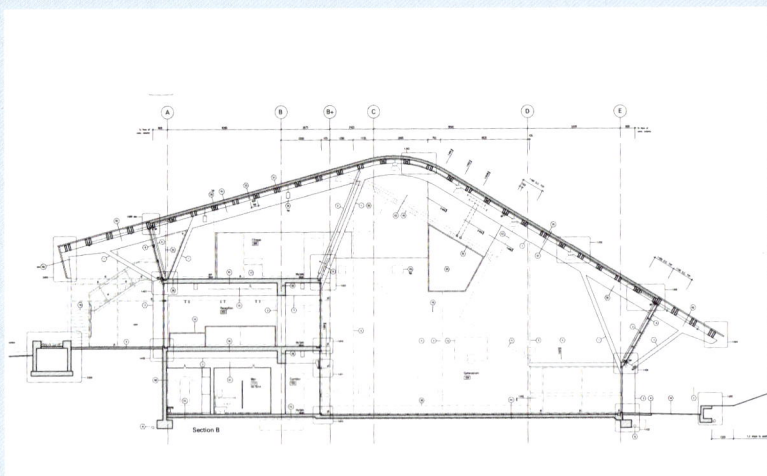

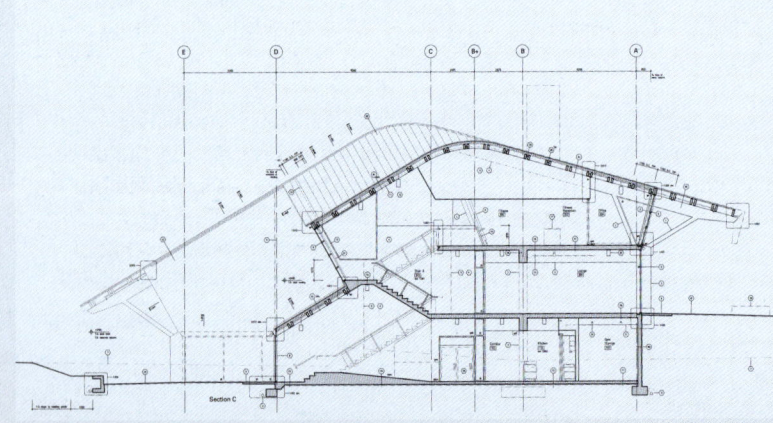

complexity. One of the most significant is the programme. And while we do not feel that complexity is necessarily a product of size, the many different requirements of this particular building – a large provincial institution located in the heart of the city of Montreal – demand that it performs in many ways. It is obviously a library but it also houses special collections and a 24-hour facility, is connected to the subway and will provide spaces for conferences, galleries and exhibitions that will become a part of the urban life of Montreal. The building is a hybrid – an invented type.

This is the largest building that we have designed and it is also our first project in French Canada – a very different place from Vancouver and one with a distinct culture. Although our office won the international competition for this project in 2000, these special conditions have prompted us to consider other ways of working. In Canada there is a culture of partnering and on this project we are collaborating with Croft Pelletier/Menkes Shooner Dagenais from Quebec. Architects from their office have come to British Columbia to work with us, and Michael Cunningham, a partner in our office who worked on the original competition, recently returned to Vancouver after living and working in Montreal for almost 12 months. These moves have helped to make our office seem less remote. They have also enabled us to work directly with the client and our French-Canadian colleagues to understand the complexities of the place and the brief and to develop the detailed design of the building from our original competition submission.

In this development of the design we have again been exploring the integration of the different systems within the building itself. So, for example, all of the servicing for the library is housed within a floor void. This has enabled us to expose almost all of the concrete structure and to use it to define parts of the building spatially while also utilising the building fabric in the conditioning of those spaces. In developing the external skin of the library we have designed it as a series of layers. Using glass, aluminium and copper, the facades have an additional outer layer of horizontal glass channels. These channels form a fixed screen that varies in density so as to offer privacy and control glare. Of course the consideration of these ideas is commonplace in Europe. However, they are less familiar in North America. Perhaps this is because of our location – there are certainly different attitudes here to the design, cost and value of buildings!

In the design of the library this varied skin forms a container that houses two other distinct containers. Both are made of wood. One, an irregular-shaped closed volume, which is located at the northern end of the building, houses the Collection Québécoise. The second, which is more open, encloses the main library stacks. And as the plan that we developed for

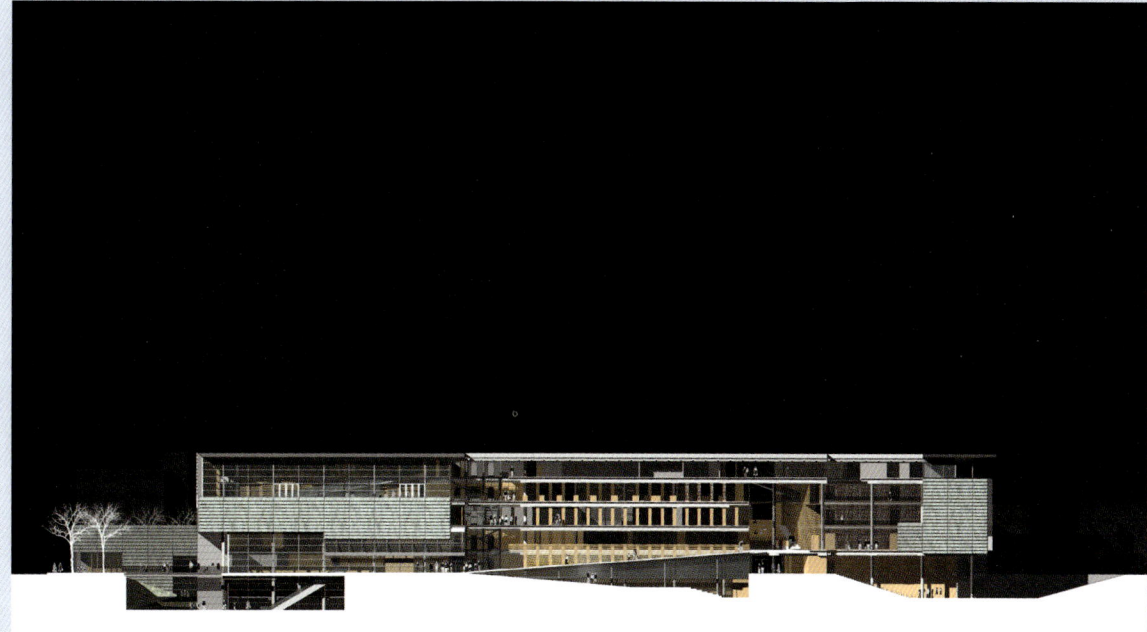

Opposite
Gleneagles Community Centre, West Vancouver, 2002

Top
Floor plan.

Middle and bottom
Sections

This page
La Grande Bibliothèque du Québec, Montreal, due for completion in 2004

Above
Cross sections.

Strawberry Vale School grouped classrooms around a path formed along the contours of the undulating ground, so this scheme also creates a path. Here it registers a conspicuously constructed ground within the building and meanders between spaces and around the two containers. In threading its way through the building this path also reveals other spaces and creates other landscapes, widening to form places for research, quiet areas and clearings where there are spaces for study. The path is an experiential device that helps to transform not only the programme but also the perception of the library.

The creation of the path and the concept of the containers contained were two ideas that were embedded in our competition-winning scheme for the library. We have found that ideas like this often begin intuitively and emerge slowly through both the body of our work and in the design of particular projects. In this respect the library, although significantly larger and more complex than the other buildings that we have designed, has projected our work into other realms of invention. The construction of the building is well under way in Montreal but of course for us the jury is out until it is completed in 2004. ⌀ BC

Patkau Architects was founded by John and Patricia Patkau in Edmonton, Canada, in 1978. In 1984 the firm relocated to Vancouver, British Columbia. Michael Cunninhgam became a partner in 1995.

Laboratoires

Nicholas Olsberg, the director of the Canadian Centre for Architecture (CCA) in Montreal, introduces 'Laboratoires', an exhibition at the CCA from April to September 2002, co-curated by Frédéric Migayrou and Mark Wigley, which invited French-Canadian architects to transfer their cultural perceptions to an international stage and engage with the wider significance of 11 September.

The poem of the mind in the act
of finding what will suffice… It
has to construct a new stage. It
has to be on that stage
And, like an insatiable actor,
slowly and
With meditation speak words
that in the ear,
In the delicatest ear of the
mind, repeat,
Exactly, that which it wants to
hear, at the sound of which, an
invisible audience listens,
Not to the play, but to itself.
— Wallace Stevens, *Modern Poetry* (1942)

Security is mostly superstition.
It does not exist in nature.
Life is an unequivocal adventure
or it is nothing
— *Helen Keller*

Historians will tell us, no doubt, that a third millennium began on or about 11 September 2001. 'Laboratoires' was designed to turn this uncertain watershed into fertile ground, bringing together two coincident forces: the sudden recognition that we need to construct a new stage for thought and action and the startling emergence in Montreal of a cluster of inventive design ateliers rooted in the idea of architecture as a language of reflection. Architecture inevitably engages with the future, gathers or disperses, sets up boundaries or bridges between possessed and dispossessed, builds walls across which to trespass or behind which to hide, constructs spaces of dialogue, conflict and congregation. The function of this project was not to predict or prophesy but to use architecture as a way of thinking, to explore patterns of possibility.

The core of 'Laboratoires' was an exhibition in which young practitioners were invited to take over the main galleries of the CCA and each create an installation that enunciated their current thinking about the world they might now inhabit and the one they might want to shape. Before these installations were realised, the architects engaged with two consulting curators, Frédéric Migayrou and Mark Wigley, and a panel of local critics and creators in dance, theatre and the visual arts to clarify, extend or focus the ideas that orient their projects. Once made, the pieces took on a second life and expression, as the public confronted them – physically and verbally – in the galleries, in public forums and on a wildly free website.

...there is ignorance on those walls, there are answers to questions that most never ask. It is the beginnings of good architecture.

...is our need for boundaries necessarily in our buildings? (visitor comments)

The project should therefore be seen as an ongoing laboratory of ideas as much as an exhibition – a year-long workshop in which curator, critic, artist and the public debate, using architecture as a common language for thinking about the future. The exhibition served not as the objective of the project but as the fulcrum for the 'intense human interaction' that founding director of the CCA Phyllis Lambert has identified as the critical generative force for new ideas in architecture today, recognising that every aesthetic project is also an act of friendship, of community.

Shelter from the Storm

A Degree Zero Architecture

Brigitte Desrochers draws a parallel between artists' response to the devastation of the Second World War and architects' reaction to the events of 11 September, as she explains how the Montreal architects participating in 'Laboratoires' responded by finding 'liberation in rubble'.

Strange how New York City turned its back on Frank Gehry's proposal for the Guggenheim headquarters after 11 September 'because it looks like the rubble'.[1] Our relation with the built environment has changed since the collapse of the World Trade Center in ways that go beyond such petty worries as who should build what on a hot piece of real estate.

Elaborating on the impetus for 'Laboratoires', co-curator Frédéric Migayrou observed at one of the workshops developing the project that European artists reacted to the Second World War 'by rehearsing destruction in their own work. They were after what was irreducible about their practice, they wanted to fold back on the basics of their medium: Roland Barthes sought a degree zero literature, the Nouveau Roman destroyed the narrative; Dubuffet tried to destroy painting, Buren brought it to its degree zero. Architects haven't done that, though. Now it is America's turn to go through this difficult rite of passage, and everyone's chance to come to terms with a degree zero practice'.

Architects and critics have been toying with the idea over recent years: ruins were already on their way to becoming a central topos in cultural theory, historians studied their relevance in modern times and architects stopped shunning decrepit buildings. They looked at obsolescence and weathering in a positive light, experimented with fragile, reactive materials and toyed with cataclysmic motifs.[2] Architecture journals showed icons of the modern movement in states of disrepair without expressing the usual outrage or making the mandatory call for restoration;[3] Sam Durant argued that, in Los Angeles, Schindler's battered and weathered Bethlehem Baptist Church was more significant, more real as it were, than the neatly restored Schindler House.[4] Tschumi applauded the decrepitude of Villa Savoye; Toyo Ito broadcast the destruction of his first signature house in a meeting of the Any Corporation,[5] admitting that he 'felt almost nothing, neither sadness, nor regret, nor even emptiness. It seemed to me that all this resulted from something far greater than personal feelings'.[6] Tschumi retaliated with x-rays of his own crushed bones. Like Ito, and like a character out of a Cronenberg movie he showed no sadness, no regret. He used ruins as an entry point into a discussion about the dynamic and perishable nature of the material world. Even before 11 September, then, architects started to let go of their reassuring corporate image.

To be sure, most people want architects to keep up the appearances of a solid and durable world order. Companies commission stately headquarters to proclaim their reliability, and newly weds buy expensive houses in order to exorcise current divorce rates. The striving for permanence in an ever-changing world remains the bread and butter of architects, but in view of recent events many have grown weary of the reassuring role society imposes upon them. Like sailors who walk on the deck of a ship with their knees bent, cutting-edge architects play the card of suppleness and adaptability. Rather than defend their old-fashioned fort they would rather edit it all down, get down to basics and travel light.

Other disasters have inspired architects to reconsider the essentials of their discipline. After a major earthquake destroyed Kobe in 1995, the Tokyo-based Workshop for Architecture and Urbanism published Ryuji Myamoto's photographs of the disaster, advising its readers: 'Take a close look at Kobe just before its reconstruction began. It may hold some clues to help us toward a re-evaluation of our investment in the city and what we look for there'.[7] These images profoundly affected Arata Isozaki, who observed: 'The composition of buildings, whose substance had been carefully hidden in order to smooth the flow of urban activities, was now revealed in its bare materiality... all became substance'.[8] Just the same, Pierluigi Nicolin dared admit that he felt a tinge of relief when he visited earthquake-damaged Belice: finally, he noted, a chance to 'start again from scratch'.[9]

Montreal architects also seem to have found liberation in rubble. When the Canadian Centre for Architecture asked them how 11 September had transformed their relationship with their medium, a single architect – Pierre Thibault – considered mourning and recovery to be the principal issues raised by 11 September, as he

put together a round structure to embrace visitors and receive their handwritten testimonies. In contrast, the collapse of the twin towers steered Atelier BRAQ into a drastic re-evaluation of the role of architecture with a strangely compelling, but ultimately crushing piece. They wedged a thick, dark wooden wall into the exhibition hall to isolate visitors from the rest of the show. Relief was provided in the form of thin openings, through which one could observe graffiti of more primitive approaches to construction. Their installation posed the question: Why is it that a building should take such a hold on us? What is it that 'we look for there', as the citizens of Kobe put it?

BUILD looked destruction in the eye, getting as close as they could to the moment of the disaster. They suspended a ton of aluminium rods in midair to form a curtain; a stream of air made the rods clang against each other. A small piece by Hexagone from the Institute of Digital Media Technology was projected in their midst – a countdown from 10 to the moment they feel is the most destructive and quite paradoxically the most productive moment in a building's life. 'We are obsessed with the immediate,' confesses BUILD co-founder Michael Carroll. Co-curator Mark Wigley adds: 'There is a tremendous intimacy between construction and destruction. Construction involves destruction, the buildings that shelter us also threaten us, but we refuse to think about it. Coming to terms with this, facing trauma in all of its actuality is the one way left open for us to get in touch with the basics of the medium'.

Walking from one installation to another amounted to a long process of shedding preconceptions, of letting go

Previous page
Pierre Thibault, 'Ecriture mémoire'.

This page
Left
Atelier BRAQ, 'Mur type: une investigation dans la parol, le lieu de l'architecture'.

Right
BUILD, 'Code Zero'.

Opposite
Boss's design.

All images: Photos Michel Legendre © Centre Canadien d'Architecture/Canadian Centre for Architecture, Montréal.

of what one would have thought was essential to the medium. After authority is gone, after meaning is gone, when there is nothing but rubble, immense and relatively untrodden ground remains to be explored. Consequently, in 'Laboratoires', architecture became process. The installation by Boss scooped raw materials up in abrupt waves and packed them all into a construction-site trailer. They were in disarray, they were full of loose ends and rough edges, they smelled. It was unclear whether these were raw materials for a landscape in the making or scraps salvaged from a demolition site. The more one wondered, the more one realised it did not really matter. The installation was about a transient state when a building is not quite done (or undone) and not quite serviceable (or no longer usable).

Likewise, Atelier in-situ's 'Test Chamber' passed from state to state in seemingly random ways, week after week. Its slick white panels opened and closed, they blocked, caught and reflected light. These conditions were recorded in a series of photographs that lined the wall adjacent to the mysterious object, like a doctor's notes pinned at the foot of the patient's bed. Atelier Big City followed suit with a piece that was not about its own physical self but about the movements and the behaviours it enabled. It dazzled visitors with its strong colours and forced everyone to clamber on and around it before they could visit the other rooms. People turned and tottered, they hesitated, they crossed over and went forward, creating a pattern of random, open-ended movements. This, to Big City, is the true nature of urbanity: cities are spaces of action, not collections of objects.

It took the sight of crowds running for their lives, of massive buildings in tatters, for the architectural community to fully come to terms with the mortality of buildings and the fragility of their trade. Before the disaster an overwhelming majority of architects were looking the other way – the way of certainties, of static and supposedly everlasting constructions. Buildings were respected. They would not consider the possibility of a degree zero architecture, even after the Second World War. The ruins that filled Europe were nowhere to be seen in the postwar architecture journals of Canada and the US. No one in their right mind would have published photographs of destroyed buildings unless they were related to research on blast-resistant architecture.[10]

However, readers who followed this research soon heard about deadly radiations that travelled out of atomic bombs, into space and through perfectly sound buildings. As the Cold War progressed, a strange new typology appeared in the architectural press: the bomb shelter. It was the ultimate, indestructible architecture. Magazines published extensively on 'atomic architecture', featuring the plans of shelters suitable for small groups, middle-sized communities or big metropolises. In 1958, Lloyd Wright combined a proposed shopping and business centre with a nuclear bomb shelter for the inhabitants of an entire community in Los Angeles, and in 1959 *Progressive Architecture* got the scoop on 'an Orwellian scheme for sheltering from bomb-blast and fallout the 4,000,000 people who live, work or visit in Manhattan'.[11] The proposal involved digging out all of Central Park, building the underground city and replanting the park over its concrete roof.

What now seems like a spectacularly eerie series of articles eventually raised an outcry. When he saw a small ad for a bomb shelter in the real-estate section of

Notes
1. Doug Saunders, *The Globe and Mail*, Saturday, 29 September 2001.
2. Among other pieces, Heinz Schütz, 'Fame + Ruins', *Architectural Design*, vol 71, no 6, November 2001, pp 54–7, and Max Kozloff, 'City of crowds, city of ruins', *Artforum*, vol XXIX, no 9, May 1991, pp 113–21; Johanne Lamoureux, 'La théorie des ruines d'Albert Speer ou l'architecture "futuriste" selon Hitler', *RACAR*, XVIII, 1–2, 1991, pp 57–63; Spiro Kostof, 'His Majesty the Pick: The aesthetics of demolition', *Design Quarterly*, 1982, pp 33–41; 'Durability and Ephemerality', *Harvard Design Magazine*, Fall 1997, with contributions by Alexander von Hoffman, Edward Ford, Ellen Dunham-Jones and Botond Bognar; Michael Milojevic, 'Time constructions, an architectural lineage of weathering steel', *Praxis*, Issue 1, vol 1, 2000, pp 44–9; Peter Salter, 'Patine et vieillissement', *L'architecture d'aujourd'hui*, no 331, Nov/Dec 2000, pp 58–63; Janet Abrams, 'Storm warning', *Lotus International*, no 79, 1993, pp 104–8; Luis Fernandez-Galliano, 'Earthquake therapy', *Lotus International*, no 104, 2000, pp 44–59.
3. Charles Bilas, 'La modernité architecturale sous bénéfice d'inventaire', *L'architecture d'aujourd'hui*, no 331, Nov/Dec 2000, pp 36–43; Wijnanda Deroo, *Arkkitehti*, vol 95, no 5, 1998, pp A18–A32.
4. Sam Durant, 'Saving graces', *Artforum*, May 2001, pp 151–2.

Above, left
Atelier in-situ Test Chamber.
Photo Michel Legendre

Above, right
Atelier Big City, Exchangeur.
Photo Alain Laforest

All images: Centre Canadien
d'Architecture/Canadian
Centre for Architecture,
Montréal.

5. At the Berlin meeting of Any
in 1997, in *Any* magazine, nos
19–20, 1997, in a conference at
the Pompidou Centre in
December 1997 and in
L'architecture d'aujourd'hui,
no 316, April 1998, pp 73–87.
6. Toyo Ito 'la villa G',
L'architecture d'aujourd'hui,
no 316, April 1998, p 82.
7. Akira Suzuki, 'Kobe 1995;
after the earthquake',
Telescope/workshop for
Architecture and Urbanism,
Tokyo 1995, p 5.
8. Arata Isozaki, 'On ruins',
Lotus International, no 93,
1996, p 39.
9. Pierluigi Nicolin, 'After the
earthquake', *Lotus
Documents*, Electa (Milan),
1983, p 127.
10. As was the case with
features in *Architectural
Forum*, November 1950, pp
146–7, and *Architectural
Record*, July 1952, pp 185–6.
11. *Progressive Architecture*,
vol 40, Jan–June, 1959, p 151.
12. *Casabella* 297, 1961, p 1.
13. Robert Smithson, 'Entropy
made visible', originally
published in *On Site*, no 4,
1973, reprinted in Jack Flam,
*Robert Smithson, the
Collected Writings*, University
of California Press (Berkeley),
1996, pp 303–9.

a Roman newspaper, Ernesto Rogers erupted: 'Surviving is not living; it only means that one is transformed into a mere, biological entity, limited to a metabolical existence and closed to the vaster, historical dimensions of living. Architecture is, conceptually, synonymous with life, and not just the life that runs through our veins, but the life that traverses past, and future generations: to make architecture is to bring the past up to the present, and to steer the present towards the future. Whoever fails to understand this fundamental principle should not be an architect'.[12] In keeping with Rogers' sentiments, a new humanist and historicist approach to architecture eventually developed into one of the most influential currents of late 20th-century architectural thinking and practice.

North America eventually reacted to the culture of control and permanence that branched out from military considerations into every sphere of public and private life – the interstate highways programme, the eradication of 'decayed' inner cities and the marketing of system controls for office buildings, air conditioners in family houses, refrigerators, plastic containers and maintenance-free materials. In the late 1960s, highway revolts erupted in San Francisco, old buildings became objects of desire and self-built cities seemed like a better option. Sick buildings and the energy crisis would add fuel to the debate.

There were few people left to think of architecture as a warlike instrument helping the march of progress when, in 1973, Robert Smithson urged architects to let go of their authoritative, controlling ways by saying: 'It's very hard to predict anything; anyway all predictions tend to be wrong… [Architects] don't take those things into account. Architects tend to be idealists, and not dialecticians… They never seem to allow for any kind of relationship outside their grand plan…so it's a rather static way of looking at things… I propose [instead] a dialectic of entropic change'.[13]

The installations at the CCA gave a measure of the distance travelled, from the necessary, protective reaction of the architecture community after the Second World War through a long awakening to the fact that demolition, ageing, death and the passing of generations remain a fundamental dimension of existence – ours, and that of buildings. Today, the profession may finally be ready to accept, and integrate these issues in theory and in practice. At the close of one of the public debates between Mark Wigley and Frédéric Migayrou that were held in conjunction with the exhibition, Mark Wigley concluded: 'There is an intimacy between construction and destruction… [with which] the architect is very familiar, but it is not yet part of our architectural discourse… It would be irresponsible for architects to continue to project their certainties out in the public realm… Any architecture that celebrates its own, let's say, fragility, is the better one. It is more reflective than an architecture that insists on its own strength… [I]t is terribly important to try and think of a way of cultivating a different role for the architect'. ⌂

Nicholas Olsberg is the director of the CCA in Montreal. He has written widely on the cultural history of North America, including contributions to the Whitney Museum's American Century project and essays on Frank Lloyd Wright, Marshall McLuhan and the American South.

Brigitte Desrochers is a Canadian architect, architectural historian and media artist trained in Montreal and at Harvard GSD. She has done extensive research on antiquarian culture in 19th-century Italy and France, particularly with regard to the early excavations in Pompei. She is currently working on a biography of Francois Mazois (1783–1826), the French archaeologist, polemist and advocate of the neo-grec.

Fleeing from an inhospitable climate and infertile land, the Vikings were intrepid explorers. However, after the Viking empire collapsed in the 14th century, Norway was ruled by Sweden and Denmark. After gaining independence in 1905, Norway guarded its autonomy by remaining neutral in the First World War but later realised that its interests would be better served by a more international outlook. Norway's quiet role within the United Nations and as international diplomat has helped to calm conflicts around the world, from the Middle East to Sri Lanka. Ironically, however, although Norwegian politicians of many persuasions have long been committed to the European Union, membership has been consistently rejected by Norway's people.

Occupying the mountainous northern edge of Europe – with nearly as much territory above the Arctic Circle as below – much of the country is sparsely inhabited and the major population centres are found along the coastal fjords.

Although Norway has benefited from a social democracy and a reasonably healthy economy during much of the 20th century, it was regarded by its wealthier Scandinavian neighbours as a poor provincial nation of farmers and fishermen. However, this perception was dramatically altered with the discovery of extensive reserves of North Sea oil and gas in Norwegian waters in 1969. Today, Norway is the third largest oil producer in the world, and with a population of just 4.5 million enjoys a high standard of living.

The government is the client for the majority of new buildings in the country. Many architects work in the public sector, and because public projects of any size are required to be commissioned through design competitions, private offices are also nourished by the system.

Although Norway was not as active as its Scandinavian neighbours in contributing to the development of Modernism, more recently it has gained prominence through the writings of Christian Norberg-Schultz and the buildings of Sverre Fehn, the only Scandinavian architect to have received the Pritzker Prize. In contrast with Fehn, whose work has been rooted in Norwegian landscape and culture, a number of the current generation of young Norwegian architects are working both in Norway and further afield.

These include Jan Olaf Jensen, who first gained international attention for the design of a leper hospital in India; Jarmund/Vigsnaes who have recently completed a house in Mallorca and are designing student housing in the Netherlands in collaboration with Bert Dirrix and Peter Zumthor; and Snøhetta, who have completed major buildings in Alexandria and Berlin – projects which have been actively supported by a government that increasingly understands that architecture is a form of international diplomacy and a valuable export.

Current projects by these architects in Norway are influenced by this international exposure, yet remain in the thrall of the compelling Norwegian landscape – in Oslo, at the Arctic Circle and beyond.

Previous page
**Mortensrud Church,
Oslo, 2002**

Jensen & Skodvin

Mortensrud Church,
Oslo, 2002

Above left
The stacked stone wall filters
light into the church, and the
rocks excavated on the site
mark the worship space.

Above right
The dry-stone wall forms a
rainscreen that is opened up to
the windows of the parish hall.

Mortensrud, a suburb in the outermost ring of
growth surrounding Oslo, is 10 kilometres from
the city centre. It is a place in transition – in the
country yet with development being spurred by
both public transportation and good road links
into the city. The new Lutheran church, designed
by Jensen & Skodvin, is only a short walk from
the subway and nearby shops. However, this
short walk is sufficient to leave the suburb
behind and place the church in a landscape of
fields and forest.

Mortensrud Church

The church and parish hall are pulled apart to create a
shared entrance court. Sited on elevated ground, the
buildings are approached on a path alongside and well
below the church. From this vantage point, the dry-
stone walls of the church, like a castle or fortification,
appear to be extensions of the rocky outcrop. The path
rises gently to arrive at the entrance court where
worshippers turn and either continue their ascent to
the church or move down into the parish hall at the low
point of the sloping court. The court is defined by a
concrete slab that is irregularly bounded on one side
by the rocky ground, and on the other where the
ground falls steeply away by a precise straight edge
and balustrade. This space between buildings is
informally occupied by the bell tower, existing pine
trees and boulders.

Moving across the forecourt, the central gabled roof
of the sanctuary is clearly visible, flanked by the slender
wooden bell tower to the left and a cubic stone volume
housing church offices on the right. This tension
between centralised symmetry and peripheral
asymmetry is reiterated throughout the scheme. The
wooden doors of the church appear to float in the low
glazed entrance facade. Inside the doors the concrete
floor continues to rise, then levels to enable the narthex
to open generously to a brick-vaulted coffee lounge on
the right. In contrast, the enclosed volume of the
confessional – unusual in a Lutheran church – is to the
left. Approached along a narrow winding ramp enclosed
by walls, the confessional brings pastor and parishioner
together on a single bench in a tiny wood-lined room
that looks out to the forest.

The transition from narthex to sanctuary is defined by two glazed exterior courts that are cut into the volume of the building. These are symmetrical about the central axis yet distinctly different in detail. One, occupied by mature trees and natural ground, is inaccessible. The other, to be occupied by people, has a slatted wood deck and opens out from the narthex and coffee lounge.

The sanctuary is defined by a freestanding steel frame with a steeply pitched gabled roof. This axial core is wrapped by a spatial band of varying width and density. On the north and west, a glazed envelope is pulled 1.5 metres away from the steel frame to create a 'light' skin, while on the east facade, a three-metre-wide 'dark' perimeter band provides both a wider side aisle on the main floor and a balcony for additional seating.

To the north behind the altar and to the west, the steel frame is infilled with dry stone at the upper level and remains open at floor level to allow views out to the forest. On the east, the frame remains predominantly open. However, instead of views, the joint between the steel frame and thick perimeter band is articulated by indirect daylight from above. The dry stone thus becomes a light-diffusing translucent screen that in its irregularity contrasts markedly with the precision of the steel frame. The translucency of the stone is enhanced by the luminance of the simple corrugated galvanised-steel ceiling of the sanctuary. The uncut stone is carefully laid to present a relatively smooth face into the sanctuary while the intentionally jagged outer faces are more closely allied with the rocky site.

The seating, aisle and altar are asymmetrically placed within the symmetrical inner volume of the church. From its high point at the entrance to the sanctuary, the floor of the church slopes almost imperceptibly down to the altar. This physical momentum is continued visually by the expansion of the interior space behind the altar out to a terrace bounded by a low wall. The altar is raised on a slim concrete slab that appears to float just 150 millimetres above the floor. The pulpit is also slightly elevated but in contrast with the altar is firmly founded on a rock that penetrates from the ground through the concrete slab.

The parish hall has been shaped by the same ordering system as the church. The central double-height meeting and social space is wrapped by a band of varying width that incorporates two floors of offices for the church and for social services, a kitchen, rooms for church groups and a warden's flat. The parish hall is clearly subordinate, not only lying below the church on the hill but entered on the return face of a projecting bay instead of axially from the front. And while the elevation of the parish hall facing the court is a double-height glazed screen, the upper storey is translucent so that from the higher vantage point of the church the eye is directed down into the hall rather than across the space on equal ground.

In contrast with the church, where windows are set flush with the outer face of the stone rainscreen cladding, the windows of the parish hall are deeply recessed with expressed galvanised-steel box lintels supported on slender staggered pipe columns. More modest wood-cladding appears on the north and east faces of the parish hall, and the rear facade, which overlooks the pasture of an adjacent farm, is entirely of wood. While it is possible to see from the entrance court through a series of interior and exterior spaces out to the woods behind the altar of the church, the parish hall provides a visual stop to this carefully constructed linear spatial sequence, offering instead views to either side.

In this scheme, Jensen & Skodvin skilfully blur the boundary between interior and exterior space. The continuity of the material palette inside and out and the superimposition of layers of transparency and translucency work well in this merging of architecture with nature. Providing both an inner sanctum and a civic space, the scheme addresses the dual task of the church to foster introspection and engagement with society. In its juxtaposition of precise and imprecise ordering systems, it also reflects a search for certainty in an uncertain world.

Mortensrud Church, Oslo, 2002

Top
Ground-floor plan.

Bottom
The church defines the edge of a rock outcrop at the outskirts of Mortensrud.

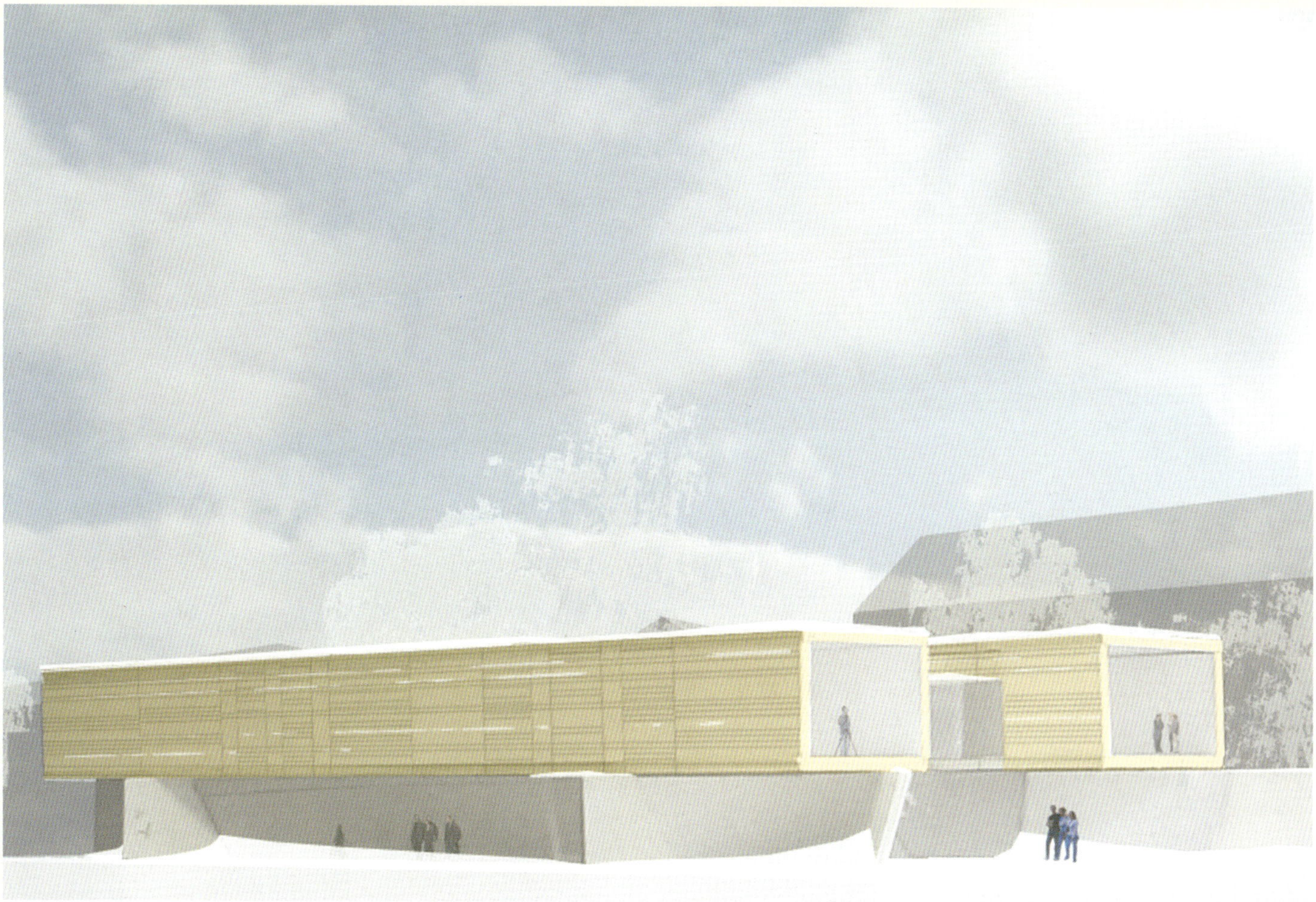

Top
The Sadje Project – Gällivare Centre, Sweden (in design development) - Wintertime view.

Bottom
The Sadje Project – Tysfjord Centre, Norway (in design development) - Summertime view.

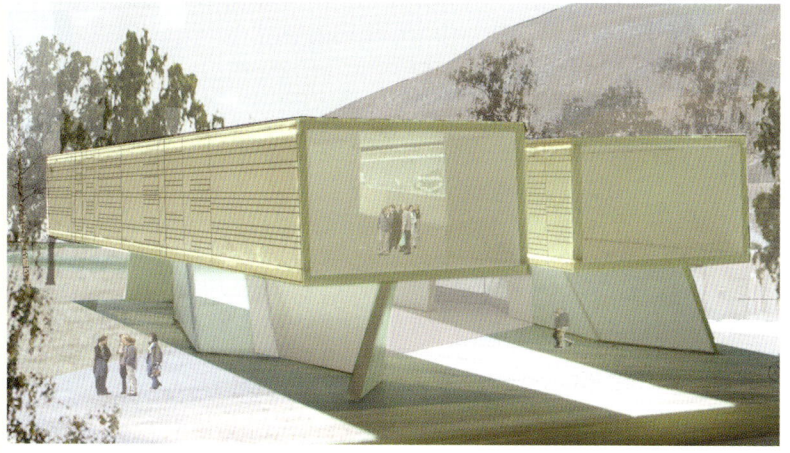

Snøhetta

Stretching across the northernmost reaches of Scandinavia and Russia, an area formerly denoted on maps as Lapland has in recent years come to be more correctly known as Sampi. This word – which in the indigenous language of the area means both the land and its people – fittingly describes some of the oldest peoples of Europe who have historically been seminomadic reindeer-herders, living near grazing lands in the interior during the winter and migrating with their animals towards the coast in the summer.

The Sadje Project

Interference with the Sami way of life began in the 17th century when Norway, Sweden and Russia began to colonise their northern lands. By the end of the 19th century Norway had banned the use of indigenous dialects in schools and required knowledge of Norwegian as a condition of owning land. However, during recent decades, as the world has become increasingly multicultural, the Scandinavian countries – like many nations with indigenous populations – have reconsidered their position. In 1988, the preservation of the Sami language and culture was incorporated as a right in the Norwegian constitution, and shortly after the Sami parliament was opened in Karasjok. These indigenous northern people now have dual citizenship in Sweden and Norway.

In 1996, the United Nations and UNESCO declared the 10,000-square-kilometre Sampi territory in northern Sweden a World Heritage Area to safeguard its unique natural, ecological and cultural traditions. Norway is currently in the process of drafting protective legislation for significant parts of its northern lands. With the international spotlight on the Sampi region, the need to gather information about and document the Sami language, culture and territories has gathered momentum. To this end, funding from the European Community enabled the neighbouring northern counties of Tysfjord in Norway and Gällivare in Sweden to embark on Interreg Atlas 2000, a digital database of Sami land and culture that is intended, together with the public libraries in the region, to be the foundation for a permanent documentation centre.

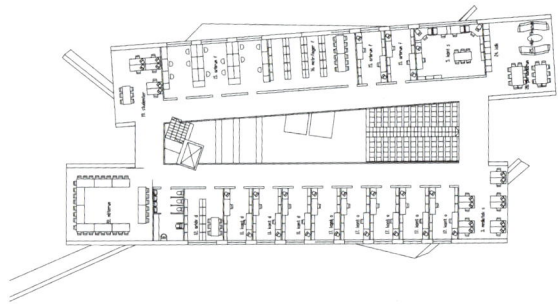

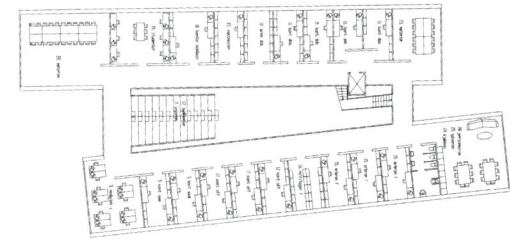

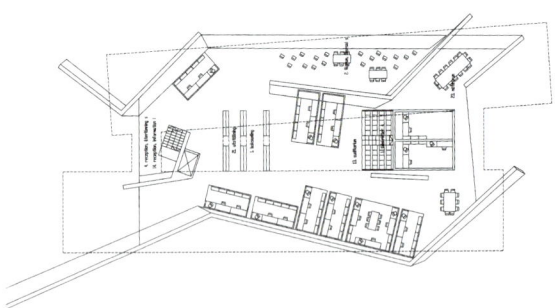

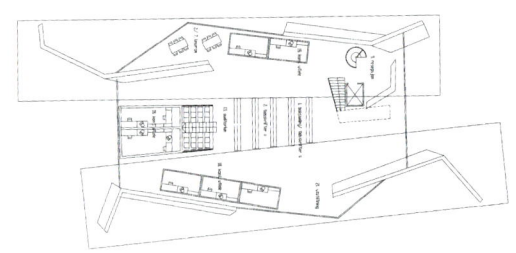

This permanent centre, currently being designed by Snøhetta working in consultation with the Sami, is being promoted as a physical symbol of this new transnational cooperation. Appropriately, the Sadje Project comprises two centres, one in Tysfjord and the other in Gällivare. Although these places are only 250 kilometres apart, they are separated by mountains into two quite distinct physical realms. Tysfjord is at the heart of the summer habitat along the coastal fjords, while Gällivare is a major town near the winter grazing lands.

The buildings are conceived as twins that are similar but not identical. Located strategically in each town, they will reinforce other existing civic functions. The key component of these modest 1500-square-metre buildings will be a *sadje*, or meeting hall. In addition, they will incorporate both a public library and a library of Sami language and culture, a documentation and information centre that will support the Interreg Atlas Project, areas for researchers working on local natural and cultural issues, a distance-learning studio and offices for Sami organisations.

The buildings are organised as two-storey volumes, with the more public functions including the library, information centre and meeting rooms at ground level, and office and research spaces on the upper floor. The two levels are to be linked by a central void in which is located the meeting hall – designed as an open amphitheatre instead of an enclosed room. The ground level of the buildings is to be defined by two linear site-cast concrete walls the cranked profile of which is inspired by the dry-stone reindeer fences that dot the landscape. These concrete walls support more pristine, abstract wood-clad orthogonal volumes above.

In order to minimise the cost of the buildings and maximise their use, their open-ended form is reiterated by a flexible concept of use. Meeting rooms on air cushions and movable stacks in the libraries can be shifted both within and outside the buildings to free up floor area for gatherings. In addition it is envisaged that the buildings will be centres for mobile libraries that will travel throughout the region.

In contrast with a number of other buildings that have sought their formal inspiration in the traditional Sami tent, or *lavvo*, the formal and material language of the twin libraries seeks to balance the culture of the region with contemporary, international construction practices. By incorporating migratory elements within the fixed building envelope, reference is made to the contradiction inherent in the contemporary condition of nomads who, now living in towns, have become more sedentary. By using sophisticated information technology to gather and disseminate local information, and providing gathering spaces where people can meet alongside distance-learning centres, the Sadje Project seeks to integrate local and global culture. By forging an alliance between digital technology and the preservation of a centuries-old way of life that intimately connects a people to the land, these twin libraries will be emblems of a culture that – formerly at the edge of our awareness – is now moving to centre stage. **Δ**

Jarmund/Vigsnaes

Headquarters for the Governor of Svalbard

The Svalbard archipelago is remote. Located 640 kilometres north of the Norwegian mainland and straddling latitude 80 degrees north, many of the islands are covered by glaciers and the soil is frozen to a depth of 500 metres. The temperature ranges from +20°C in summer to –50°C in winter.

Reputed to have been discovered in the 12th century by Icelandic seamen, the islands were inhabited only intermittently by fishermen until the discovery of rich coal deposits attracted the American-owned Arctic Coal Company, founded in 1906, to mine in the archipelago. Russia and Sweden also established mining operations soon after, and following the First World War Norway was granted sovereignty over the islands on the condition that these foreign operations be allowed to continue. As a consequence of their strategic importance, the mines were heavily bombarded by the Germans in the Second World War, and after the war the coal industry steadily declined. Svalbard – with its dramatic, largely untouched Arctic landscapes and abundant marine and wildlife – is now looking to adventure tourism and research to provide a more diversified economic base.

Today only Spitzbergen, the main island of the archipelago, is inhabited with a handful of settlements. Situated in the middle of the island on a narrow coastal plain at the foot of the

mountains, Longyearbyen – the largest settlement with a population of 1000 – is the seat of Norwegian government in the archipelago. After the administration building for the governor of Svalbard burned down in 1996, the Oslo-based architects Jarmund/Vigsnaes were commissioned to design a new building that would incorporate an expanded and unusual mix of public functions including government offices for the overseeing of both the mining industry and tourism, a library, flats for government officials, a prison cell and a control centre for emergency rescue operations.

To accelerate the construction programme, the reinforced concrete structure that survived the fire was reused. This frame has been wrapped with a new 'overcoat' designed around a canted geometry that satisfies the requirement for increased area while avoiding the need to construct new foundations – a costly operation because of the permafrost. The L-shaped plan of the former building has been modified by the addition of a freestanding garage for snowmobiles and rescue vehicles which marks the southeast corner of a new south-facing parking court. Low overhanging eaves provide sheltered walkways to the entrance, which is located at the knuckle of the L. In contrast with the entrance court, the roof rises up to the exterior faces of the building, which are fractured by a new double-height triple-glazed entrance foyer that provides a panoramic view of the fjord below.

Through its massing, the scheme thus makes the transition from human scale to the scale of the landscape. This transition is also supported by the two-layered envelope of the building. Punctured openings in the weather-tight inner wall clearly denote the two storeys of accommodation within, while the sculpted

Headquarters for the governor of Svalbard, Svalbard archipelago, 1998

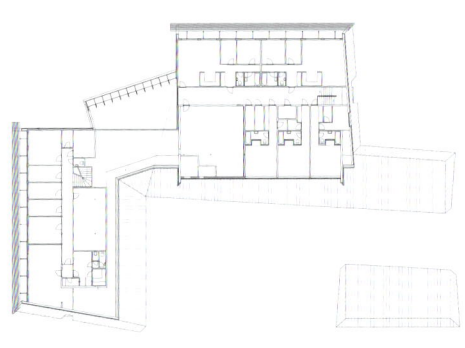

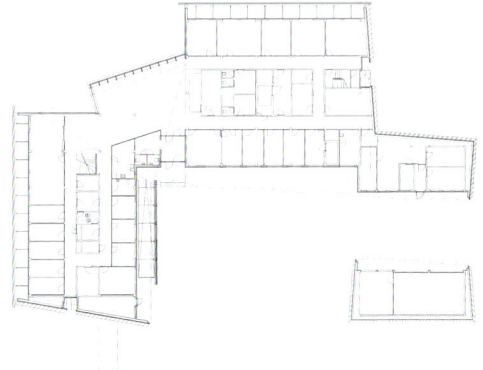

Headquarters for the governor of Svalbard, Svalbard archipelago, 1998

Above
The building is set in an expansive landscape marked by former coal-mining structures.

Below
First-floor and ground-floor plans.

overcoat – like the landscape in which size and distance are difficult to gauge – is more ambiguous. Responding to a climate in which the wind blows fiercely in all directions and drives weather horizontally, roof and walls alike are clad with pre-weathered zinc. This strategy also reinforces the monolithic reading of the building and during construction helped to minimise the number of building trades that had to be imported from the mainland.

While the use of wood is unremarkable in many places in the world, it is exotic in the treeless landscape of Svalbard. However, wood has historically been imported to the islands and was used extensively in the construction of coal-mining structures. Because wood does not rot in this very cold climate, the landscape is consequently dotted with many of the remains of these structures from the heyday of mining. The new administration building acknowledges this history. The only new foundations required were for the entrance foyer. These were made in the traditional way by drilling a hole six feet deep, inserting an untreated timber pile and filling the hole with water. Like the former building, the concrete ground slab – supported on concrete columns on the wood piles – is consequently raised from 450 to 1200 millimetres above ground to create a ventilated air-space under the building so that heat from inside does not melt the permafrost, which would cause subsidence.

Internally the building is not a typical Norwegian office building but instead – like the spartan summer camps that are a part of every Norwegian's childhood experience – has been designed to have a rough character that is appropriate to both mining and adventure tourism. The glue-laminated timber structure of the entrance foyer is complemented by plywood interior finishes, and the building's zinc overcoat gives way to canted 2 x 8 external timber screens. While these screens do provide some shading from the summer sun, their primary function is to provide a sense of mental protection. During the four months of polar night when the sun never rises above the horizon, light from within the building is reflected by the changing patterns of snow and ice on the screens, providing both a view and a sense of enclosure.

Situated above the town and overlooking the fjord, the new administration building is a beacon of civilisation that quietly asserts the presence of the state of Norway and its role in steering this remote place through the transformation from heavy industry to a new economy. To further signal its support, and in response to expanding scientific activity in the Svalbard archipelago, the Norwegian government has now commissioned Jarmund/Vigsnaes to design a centre for atmospheric and environmental research in Longyearbyen. ᗪ AWL

'At this point I can cut out the mass where the shadow screens the construction. This gives me my place, and time stands still.'

'Outside, the tree fractures the horizon. Time will allow it to grow and add to its room. The tree mobilises light and casts its shadow on the earth, a realisation of place… It is here the story is told.'

— Sverre Fehn 1981[1]

Confrontation, Limits and Fracture:

The Invention of Site in Sverre Fehn's Hamar Museum

The Norwegian architect Sverre Fehn, who has worked almost exclusively in Scandinavia, received only a 'belated recognition' for his architecture. **Suzanne Ewing** explains how Fehn's 'poetic, sculptural, humanistic and inclusive' work rested largely on his formulation of 'the invention of site', as best exemplified by the Archbishopric Museum at Hamar in Norway.

Notes
1. C Norberg-Schulz and G Postiglione, *Sverre Fehn Works, Projects, Writings 1949–1996*, Monacelli (New York), 1997, p 243.
2. The Archbishopric Museum at Hamar, Norway, 1967–79, started when Fehn was 43 and, completed when he was aged 55, is built over an archaeological site, significant in the late Middle Ages as it lay along the Kaumpung trail which was the route of the bishop of Hamar's journey to Rome in 1302. The remains of an early 19th-century farm structure rest on the top of the ruins of a medieval fortress, demolished in the second half of the 16th century. The building has been well documented, see Norberg-Schulz and Postiglione, op cit, pp 129–44, with bibliography of articles 1975–94 on p 138; also 'Hamar Bispegard Museum', GA Document No11, 1984 pp 72–81; R Weston, 'Nordic light', *Architects Journal*, no 30, September 1987, pp 25–9.
3. S Fehn, 'L'albero e l'orizzonte' (The Tree and the Horizon), *Spazio & Societa* 10, 1980, pp 32–55; P Cook, 'Trees and horizons: the architecture of Sverre Fehn', *Architectural Review*, August 1981, pp 102–6; PO Fjeld, 'The fall of horizon', in *Sverre Fehn: The Thought of Construction*, Rizzoli (New York), 1983; R Weston, 'A sense of the horizon', *Architects Journal*, 19 November 1988, pp 38–46; S Fehn, 'Above and below the horizon', *A&U*, no 1 (340), January 1999.
4. From award speech by Sverre Fehn '...about Sverre Fehn', Sverre Fehn Pritzker Architecture Prize Laureate, Los Angeles: The Hyatt Foundation, 1997, also www.pritzkerprize.com/svbio.htm
5. Cook, op cit, p 102.
6. Norberg-Schulz and Postiglione, op cit, p 19.
7. A Khan, 'Overlooking: a look at how we look at site or...site as "discrete object" of desire', in D McCorquodale, K Ruedi and S Wigglesworth, *Desiring Practices*, Black Dog Publishing (London), 1996, pp 174–85.
8. A Roy, 'Traditions of the modern: a corrupt view', in *Traditional Dwellings & Settlements Review*, vol XII, no 11, 2001, pp 7–19.
9. S Holl, *Anchoring*, Princeton Architectural Press (New York), 1989, p 11. 'A building has one site. In this one situation, its intentions are collected. Building and site have been interdependent since the beginning of Architecture. In the past, this connection was manifest without conscious intention through the use of local materials and craft, and

Introduction: Horizons and Trees

Following the completion of the Archbishopric Museum at Hamar, Norway, in 1979,[2] numerous references to 'horizon' and 'trees' appeared both in the architect Sverre Fehn's own writings and in publications about his work by others.[3] The image of the tree fracturing the horizon is important, both in defining conceptual and physical limits in relation to a particular place such as the Hamar Museum, and more broadly as an architectural device fundamental to the choreography and ordering of inhabited spaces. It can be seen to relate directly to the concept of architecture as captured space or realised place. Sites are always to some extent invented. The invention of site in Fehn's work is a significant element of his process of making architecture and therefore in the experiencing, understanding and interpretation of his buildings where 'the story is told'.

Sverre Fehn suggests that his work has come of age 'in the shadow of modernism'.[4] His built work, mainly in Scandinavia and recognised by the 1997 award of the Pritzker Prize, has been described as poetic, sculptural, humanistic and inclusive. Following exposure early in his career in the 1950s with the publishing of the Nordic Pavilion in Venice, wider acclaim for his work was consolidated in the 1980s and 1990s. Peter Cook, who in 1981 included Fehn's work in a series on 'unappreciated architects', noted: 'In Sverre Fehn we have a believing architect, and we ignore his quiet and lyrical approach to modern architecture at our peril'.[5] Fellow Norwegian Christian Norberg-Schulz commented in 1997 that: 'the belated recognition of Fehn is due to the fact that his works suddenly appear to "adapt" themselves to the international situation and to offer compelling answers to difficult and complex conditions'.[6]

The Invention of Site

It has been suggested that the subject of site has been 'systematically ignored by both architectural and urban design discourse',[7] and also to some extent is subject to fabricated dualisms inherent in modernism:[8] before/after; above/below; new/old; urban/landscape. The writings of Steven Holl are preoccupied with the anchoring of buildings in their sites. He argues: 'Architecture is bound to situation... The site of a building is more than an ingredient in its conception. It is its physical and metaphysical foundation... Today the link between site and architecture must be found in new ways, which are part of the constructive transformation of modern life'.[9]

Andrea Kahn observes that we are usually 'in the midst of site' rather than 'hovering over', as in most modernist conceptions.[10] She unravels the myth of the contained and controllable site, an assumed 'blank canvas' that requires erasure or cleansing, and challenges the assumption that analysis is merely a scientifically objective, neutral description of data. She suggests instead that interpretation, assumption and invention are critical to how an architect responds to a particular place.

Similarly, David Leatherbarrow notes in *The Roots of Architectural Invention* that 'the existence of a defined building site is always taken for granted in contemporary architectural design, yet attempts to understand the reasons underlying its definition are surprisingly rare'.[11] He presents three contemporary partial understandings or assumptions: site as a division of space, site as context and site as real estate. Like Kahn, Leatherbarrow argues that site in relation to the act of building is always a matter of invention. He cites examples such as Alberti and the notion of site platform that may order and limit vertically, and the mediating, staged sites of Borromini that influenced the external configuration of spaces adjacent to a site, as different from Modernist notions. He cites early Modernist experiments with axonometric projection, such as that of van Doesberg, as being aimed at removing 'the composition from the horizon of perspectival experience, which confers frontality on whatever (object or person) reciprocates the "frontalism" of one's body'. This abstraction dislocates from real time, with the potential confusion of horizon and perspective, or vista, as 'a view on reality' rather than understood implicit presence.

Two well-known 20th-century images come to mind.[12] The first is Le Corbusier's 'eye of man to see a wide horizon', constructed in the grass-floored 'room' on the roof of the de Bestegui apartment in Paris (1932), which, by maximising the sense of being in a room beneath the vast expanse of the sky, effectively obscures the urban landscape of Paris except for a top slice of the monumental Arc de Triomphe in the background. The context is edited to enhance the oscillation between fireplace and triumphal arch, imbuing a sense of the partially bounded white-walled room encircled by an imaginary territory marked by the city monument. The second is the roofscape of the Unité d'Habitation in Marseilles (1945–52) where sculptural forms are set against the clean horizon of the mountains and clear sky in the background, the whole on an elevated plane or platform. There is a heightened sense in these two images of what is near or far and of the bounding of a room located in relation to a surrounding horizon. The Modernist conception Kahn notes of 'hovering over' is combined with some sense of Holl's 'expression linked to idea joined to site'.

Heidegger's rethinking of the nature of space, place and inhabitation is also relevant. His work from the late 1920s to the 1960s freed the question of space from its previous disciplinary boundaries, breaking from a

Cartesian ontology of neutral, flattened space – site as a division of space – and reasserting investigation into the spatiality of the world in which we find ourselves, 'the concrete context of actual life'. Heidegger's concepts of *horismos* and *raum* have been noted as a preoccupation of Fehn's work.[13] Heidegger observes: 'What the word for space, raum, designates is said by its ancient meaning. Raum means a place cleared or freed for settlement and lodging. A space is something that has been made room for, something that is cleared and free, namely within a boundary, Greek peras. A boundary is not that at which something stops but, as the Greeks recognised, the boundary is that from which something begins its presencing. That is why the concept of horismos, that is the horizon, the boundary. Space is in essence that for which room has been made, that which is let into bounds'.[14]

Confrontation and Control
Confrontation and struggle are recurrent themes of language used by Fehn in his narratives where, 'acting violently in order to emphasise... latent, secret, hidden qualities', he calls the act of building 'brutal'. Fehn says: '[W]hen I build on a site in nature that is totally unspoiled, it is a fight, an attack by our culture on nature. In this confrontation I strive to make a building in the setting, a hope for a new consciousness to see the beauty there as well'.[15] Analogies with ships and conquest recur in Fehn's writings, as do his diagrams of the line of a boat forging through the sea. The implicit analogy of conquest can be read as a male–female interaction, with the site viewed as potentially fertile for building.[16]

There is resonance here with both Norwegian tradition and the Vitruvian identification of sites, as described by Leatherbarrow, where the soil is literally ploughed and cut to mark off a site from its surrounding expanse, and the resulting boundary wall denotes 'not a line but a container symbolically equivalent to the wall of a ceramic jar or vase, a limit that served as a receptacle of civic life, generative and abundant because female'. The horizon 'without' was perceived as an open expanse, an unbounded and formless field, perhaps analogous to the sea. The notion that the boat sailed to 'fight the horizon'[17] to some extent reveals a fabricated Modernist dualism of nature versus culture, with an implication that the marking vessel is the focus in undifferentiated ground rather than the balancer of territory enclosed or exposed, within or without.

Fehn refers to 'the dramatic confrontation between earth and sky. The point of intersection',

Archbishopric Museum, Hamar, 1979

Above
In juxtaposing old and new the museum documents the passing of time.

Page 93
Sverre Fehn's sketch of the concept of tree and horizon at the Nordic Pavilion in the Giardini, Venice, 1962.

noting that '[In those days] the horizon was an instrument of architecture determining the large exterior "room". The vista then served the practical purpose of defense, extending no further than the eye could see. The sight on the weapon was an extension of the eye and its view was a definition of mortality... The conversation with nature was not based on aestheticism or sentimentality, for every opening not only admitted light, but also determined survival in relation to topography'.[18] It is perhaps not surprising that invention of site begins to resonate with instrumental thinking, or military overtones, as well as perceived notions of 'primitive' attitudes to surroundings. 'Survival in relation to topography' recalls the act of building as primal confrontation with nature.

Fehn understands architecture as 'subject to the layout of the ground'. He observes that 'Sites...contain in their profundity the sense of the project, to which the architecture must conform'. Closest perhaps to Leatherbarrow's category of partial understanding of site as context, Fehn describes site as an archive distanced from the present and future, a source of information and knowledge, perhaps to be plundered, and certainly to be discovered. At Hamar, Fehn is conscious of the paradox of intervention, saying that 'the past is suddenly present, the stones come close to you, the ruins look more material and real, because they make up a story at the same time as they are attacked'.[19] In keeping with the myth of the untouched site identified by Andrea Kahn, Fehn to a certain extent invents the site at Hamar as untouched prior to the museum intervention in order to enhance this 'confrontation'.

The building was described in the 1997 Pritzker Prize proceedings as 'A suspended itinerary...overhanging... [that] reveals the story of the passing of time, the unchanging pursuit of its course, the confrontation between old and new'. John Hedjuk has described the place as 'a site where the frozen earth grips in its vise the retaining and foundation walls of past acts and occurrences. The present archaeologist reveals the earth-encrusted tombs of past joys and of past sadness. We know we are in the presence of an event and we are strangely enough participating spectators. The lake and the mountain are the proscenium'.[20] Peter Cook describes Hamar as 'a poised machine in its purest form hanging above the archaeology... [W]e are unused to a building that collages together devices, as in the tradition of the clockmaker, so that they seem naturally interdependent'. In describing Fehn's mandate as choreographer, Cook further observes that 'the whole has a fascinating violence in its configuration'.[21]

The site at Hamar – an archaeological site that incorporates medieval and 19th-century buildings, remains and artefacts – is clearly one that has been previously touched. Fehn's approach of built detachment from the past exaggerates to some extent the

by an association of the landscape with events of history and myth... Ideas cultivated from the first perception of the site, meditations upon initial thoughts, or a reconsideration of existing topography can become the framework for invention. This mode of invention is focused through a relative space, as distinct from universal space. It is in a bounded domain.'

10. Khan, op cit, pp 176–8. Kahn develops a model of Site Constructions in architectural education which acknowledge the interpretative reality of engagement with a particular physical location which is also a conceptual construction.

11. D Leatherbarrow, *The Roots of Architectural Invention, Site, Enclosure, Materials*, Cambridge University Press (Cambridge), 1993, p 7. 'We have largely missed the creative aspect of site definition and the architect's responsibility to "invent" the site of any design project.'

12. Illustration nos 46 and 47 in *Le Corbusier: Architect of the Century*, Hayward Gallery exhibition catalogue, Arts Council of Great Britain, Balding & Mansell, 1987 pp 138–9.

13. K Frampton, 'The constructive thought', in Norberg-Schulz and Postiglione, op cit, pp 253–5. Frampton links Louis Kahn and Sverre Fehn to Heidegger's distinction between evenly divided and distant space.

14. Heidegger, 1954, quoted in C Macann (ed) *Critical Heidegger*, Routledge (London), 1996.

15. Pritzker Architecture Prize Laureate 1997, op cit.

16. Cook, op cit, p 104, describes Fehn's approach to the proposed 1972 National Museum of Fine Arts: 'the city floor is not touched. The new structure "fertilises" the old. The gentle slope of the bridges activate the pedestrian's view...a city floor full of life and activities'.

17. Fjeld, op cit, p 256.

18. Fjeld, 'The precision of place', in *The Thought of Construction*, Rizzoli (New York), 1983, p 256.

19. From 'An architectural autobiography', in *The Poetry of the Straight Line: Five Masters of the North*, Helsinki, Museum of Finnish Architecture, 1992, quoted in Norberg-Schulz and Postiglione, op cit, p 246.

20. Quoted in Norberg-Schulz and Postiglione, op cit, p 257.

21. Cook, op cit, p 106.

22. F Dastur, 'The ekstatico-horizonal constitution of

interpretation of confrontation between old and new, stillness and movement, ground and sky. Movement through new spaces above or below the historic ground, combined with the ramps and gradually sloping floors of interior spaces and bridges, is carefully choreographed. Shifts of movement are articulated within constructed horizons that are fractured by stairs, the main ramp and other elements in the making of interior and exterior rooms for the new occupation.

Limits and Landscape

Norberg-Schulz outlines a narrative interpretation of the forming of limits and boundaries in relation to building: firstly, the earth as given territory; secondly, the marking or making of lines related to cultivation; and thirdly, enclosure or the containing of inhabited space. In Leatherbarrow's Vitruvian ordering of territory, the line of cut ground primarily separated different presences. In Fehn's work, ordering moves set up confrontations between nature and man, earth and sky, boat and sea. Architecture becomes a charged void contained or bounded in opposition to all that surrounds it in nature. Thus the focus is on the line or actual boundary itself – on the vessel or architectural space – rather than on the differentiated ground where it is situated.

Despite its usual meaning of a circular visual limit, the term horizon is not originally connected to seeing and intuition. 'It means, in accordance with the Greek verb *horizein*, what limits, surrounds, encloses'.[22] As the apparent line that divides the earth and the sky, it is the aspect of imagined or interpreted horizon which is pertinent to site invention.[23] The defined limits of the Hedmarkmuseet site stem from previous inhabitation, previously defined buildings and edges. Where territory is less clearly defined in the semi-enclosed courtyard excavation area, a new

visitors' ramp of the same geometrical configuration as the remains of one boundary wall is introduced in a shifted plan location. The ramp, which contains visitor movement, becomes a line cutting through the invented space bounded by the more solid wings of the museum. In moving along this ramp, Fehn suggests that: 'When the ground becomes history: man's position leaves the horizon as the bridge brings him in a state of looking down at the ornamental walls from the middle ages. All answers are given by his position in relation to the earth and the sky'.[24]

The new spaces of the Hamar Museum are deliberately positioned within the surrounding northern landscape of mountains and lake. The external ramp's furthest point from the entrance reveals a view of the wider surroundings. Although unlike the Corbusian examples noted earlier, this is a position of 'hovering over' and has analogies with the theatre of Borromini's staged, mediated sites rather than with Alberti's concept of bounded platform.[25] If the ramp in the Hamar Museum is interpreted as a container, or vessel within wider territory, it can also be seen as a partial boundary allowing the external courtyard to be understood as a series of overlapping spaces within the wider landscape. Just as the shadow of the tree realises a place on earth, or conversely makes a place real, the impact of the ramp within the building and the courtyard gives the internal and external spaces their 'being'.

Telling a Story

The simple linear buildings of the museum, defined by a timber pitched roof and masonry base, recall the basic form of Norwegian folk buildings. Spatial organisation of the galleries, where the museum of peasant life is housed, emphasises the linearity of the 19th-century low-level barns, which are perpendicular to the entrance block. Two levels are joined by a sloping concrete floor that appears to float within the space in which the existing stone walls below and the new timber post and beam frame above are differentiated. There is an ambiguity between the relative importance of lower and upper levels, one connected with the temporality', in Macann, op cit, p 164.

23. D Veseley, 'Introduction', *eric parry architects 1*, Black Dog Publishing (London), 2002, describes, 'The deeper meaning of horizon has its origin in the experience of the imaginary line where the earth meets the sky. The nature of this imaginary horizontal line is revealed in its power to define the boundary of our visible world as well as in the invitation to transcend this boundary', concluding that horizon is significant in its ability to preserve constancy of human situations.

24. *Fehn, Signs & Insights*, Urbino, 1979, quoted in Cook, op cit, p 105.

25. Weston, 'Nordic light', op cit, p 29 links the parti of this building with Corbusian vocabulary and '*promenade architecturale*'.

26. Frampton cites four primary relationships noted by Holl: under, in, on and over the earth, 'the surface of earth as self-evident but fundamental datum', in Holl, op cit, p 7.

27. Postiglione in Norberg-Schulz and Postiglione, op cit, p 58 on Hamar and the Wasa museum competition project.

28. Quoted in Norberg-Schulz and Postiglione, op cit, p 257.

Archbishopric Museum, Hamar, 1979

Opposite left
Relief plan model showing upper floor levels and courtyard ramp above existing ground, with the gallery wing on the left.

Opposite right
Sketch by Suzanne Ewing of compressed space of entrance with glimpses from excavated ground to new roof structure.

Top
The museum defines three sides of the courtyard, with the fourth opening to the landscape beyond.

Right
The view across the museum courtyard to the main ramp.

revealed depth of the earth, the other with the light and rhythm of the sky.

In the entrance area, the unresolved fusion of the existing medieval fort walls that have been incorporated into the 19th-century farm buildings can be clearly seen. The new entrance is directly opposite a major opening into the external courtyard, with a view of the new ramp which re-bounds the exterior space. The ground is revealed as uncertain. What was assumed as ground level at the entrance is contradicted by the deepening rough stone trenches that become evident as you move through the building. The smooth concrete bridge linking the gallery areas to the external ramp and its pivot stair provides a higher level datum for the insertion of concrete boxes containing especially valued objects and fragments extracted from the rough ground below. Space appears to be compressed at ground level by these monolithic, vertically oriented insertions in the space. The focus is on the cave-like quality of the excavated ground area, which recalls the underground feeling of the Venice pavilion.

Materials are used to orient human experience in relation to both ground and sky. Throughout the building the fundamental relationship of being 'above' accentuates the experience of being 'below'.[26] Within the stone walls of the museum, the transition between above and below consistently relates to penetrating light and concrete finish as seen in the stairs, the ramp and in places where what seems to be floor is articulated as bridge, allowing interaction between the two overlapping spaces. Although the highest part of the walls in the central entrance block relates to the highest point of the ramp in the courtyard, Fehn's conceptual 'point of intersection' in this building relates to the inserted routes of platform, ramp and stairs rather than the material datum between wall and roof. All below is treated as part of the dark, cave-like rough terrain. Above is the even rhythm of the articulated timber frame.

Two less apparent spaces above and below are created by the bold introduction of the ramp in the courtyard. The existing ground is read as one area bounded by the wings of the museum and located within the wider context of the lake and mountains beyond. On arrival at the lowest level, a more interior space related to the entrance of the museum is experienced, enclosed by the partial bounding of the ramp's turn. In contrast with the medieval walls, this 'space below' is not an enclosed fortress-like space but one where the wider archaeological site and landscape beyond the museum wings are emphasised. As Postiglione observes: '[T]he project culminates in the development of a route that, uncoiling itself in space, seeks to discover a new horizon'.[27] It is only from the highest point externally of the ramp that a sense of the larger space beyond the Hamar buildings is revealed.

The fundamental shift, expressed through the plan geometry and form of the ramp, is from being a protective boundary separating within from without, to being an open route, a line cutting through unbounded territory. The ramp, which carries visitors on a spatial journey around the museum, is also fundamental to the reinvention of the perceived boundaries of the new museum site. The ramp's slope by definition is about movement and the oscillating relationship between suspended route and historic ground. It can therefore also be seen as the line of intersection between the two 'rooms' of the courtyard.

Moving through the spaces of the museum, participation in the charged void between above/ below, earth/sky is accentuated by various moments of 'fracture'. At the place where the ramp penetrates the building at high level, vertical proportions and vertical elements invert the spatial horizontality of the other areas of the building. The ramp's puncture of the building adjacent to the spiral stair can therefore be interpreted as a vertical pivot or fracture, the place of real spatial shift from the end of the linear barn to the outdoor *raum*.

Fracture

Returning to the image of the tree fracturing the horizon, Fehn claims that it is in the fracturing of horizon that place can be realised. A narrative of pure or original nature is embodied in the line of the horizon where spatial infinity is inferred to be analogous with timelessness and the purity of the untouched. Interventions – the shade of the tree, the support of a column, the corner or edge of a room, the beginning of a building – serve to transform, conquer, change and fracture both space and time to enable human inhabitation.

Fehn claims his architecture attempts to provide 'a horizon for man' so that each project identifies a place between earth and sky, *mellomron* or 'the space between' in Norwegian. The 'point of intersection' or 'fracture' of what is understood physically and conceptually as horizon is fundamental to the act of inventing and making the spaces between, and it also allows opportunity to redefine the horizons of earth and sky. At Hamar, the surface of the earth is revealed as having historic depth, and the sky's potential to cast shadows is exploited. An ordering is choreographed in which the new raised ground of the contained ramp is established between the redefined horizontal datum of the roof and uneven stone remains.

Fehn's interpretation of horizon draws together an elemental understanding of human beings, building and situation, and can be argued to some extent to relate to aspects of Heidegger's philosophical approach to time and being. However, Fehn's imagined horizon is primarily spatial and physical. He notes: 'What was especially lost was the horizon, which human beings forgot with the discovery of the roundness of the earth. And with the loss of horizon we also lost known and unknown space. We have lost the earth underneath the sky and what is beyond... Let the people in their individual homes own the horizon. Let the apartment roof be the large piazza...for a visual conversation with the elements of the sky'.[28]

Conclusion

The horizon is seen by Fehn as critical to understanding the invention of site. The site at Hamar is reinvented as untouched – despite the archaeological material that is integral to its existence – and thus to some extent concurs with Modernist myths related to site. However, the insertion of new layers of ground and the roof construction enables the resulting place to eloquently develop a series of new relationships relating to space 'above' and 'below'. The articulation and manipulation of concrete and light within these new vessels, or lines of occupation, creates a charged void between earth and sky, a positioning of experience in relation to the visible horizon bounded by the rebuilt stone and timber structure, and also to the imagined boundary of the horizon.

Within the existing boundary walls of the archaeological remains, the ramp emphasises a new orientation, a line inserted into free terrain. The ramp places the visitor to some extent outside or beyond an interpreted sequence of history. A fracture at the point of pivot of the ramp's junction with the upper-level walkway and the spiral stair provides the vertical fixing point of the platforms of the interdependent museum spaces. In the Hedmarkmuseet, Fehn manipulates the horizon in terms of physical limits and experience and uses horizon as an instrument of orientation, movement and engagement. The literal 'realising of the place' is finally a process of participation on location in the reinvented site. ⌂

Suzanne Ewing is an architect who graduated from Cambridge University in 1992. She worked in practice with Page & Park in Glasgow and taught at the School of Architecture, Planning and Landscape Architecture at the University of Newcastle from 1998 until 2002. Currently she is teaching at Edinburgh University and works in practice with Zone Architects. Her writing has been published in *Scroope*, the *DoCoMoMo Journal* and most recently in the *Journal of Architecture*.

Inside to Outside/ Centre and Edge

Located in uptown Manhattan, the office of Tod Williams and Billie Tsien is at the very hub of the Western world. Here they explain how a sense of 'centre' and 'edge', as illustrated by the bronze facade for the Museum of American Folk Art (MAFA) in New York, is essential for maintaining a balance between 'problem solving' and the more creative urges in their work.

In matters of creativity architects are drawn to conditions of centre and edge. We seek centres because we are problem solvers acting in the present and operating within a cultural and architectural heritage. Our unobtainable goal is truth. Our possible goal is eloquent resolution.

We are drawn to the edge through restlessness, emotion and curiosity. Our desire is to extend our horizons.

Solving problems (or finding centres) cannot be accomplished without a sense of the perimeter, the limit and the edge. Probing horizons requires turning one's back on the centre. Nearly all of an architect's energy is devoted to solving the problem, seeking the centre. Patient (or impatient) creative search requires an appreciation of the duality, if not the tension, of centre and edge.

The design of the facade for the Museum of American Folk Art in New York may be understood as an example of both seeking the centre and the edge. We do not like to think of ourselves as facade makers. As architects we want a building to enrich experience rather than affix an image. However, an important part of the brief for the museum was to create an image and that necessitated a strong facade. MAFA had been housed in a brownstone and then behind a small storefront within a large commercial building in Manhattan for over 30 years and consequently had no visual identity. The site for the new building was 40 feet in width. Facing 53rd Street, it is surrounded on three sides by the Museum of Modern Art (MOMA). MOMA's addition, designed by Yoshio Tanaguchi, will be 30 times the size of MAFA. Thus it was essential that the new museum have a significant facade addressing 53rd Street.

Folk art, or art created by untrained artists, is still very much in the process of being understood. It is above all a personal and idiosyncratic art made by extraordinary/ordinary people. As this 'art of the people' is often under-appreciated, it required a strong creative solution to measure up to the adjoining street – 53rd between 5th and 6th Streets – which contains extraordinary architecture by Eero Saarinen, Cesar Pelli, Edward Durell Stone, Philip Johnson, Kevin Roche, Goodhue and Cram, and Tanaguchi.

Our concept for MAFA's facade was the abstraction of a mask and an open hand. The facade is primarily opaque so that light from the south does not overwhelm or damage the art within. It is also canted to catch shafts of light entering the canyons of 53rd Street in the early morning, at midday and later in the afternoon. It is set in advance of the entry doors and store-front, putting them in shadow. Slot windows between facets allow visitors glimpses of the street life below.

In concept and in construction the facade is a contemporary screen, much like any stone- or metal-clad building enclosure. The main weather barrier and the vapour barrier are independent of the cladding, enabling the outer face to act as a first line of defence against the weather.

It was essential to our concept that the opaque material for the facade be both ordinary and extraordinary. It was important that the material be reflective to catch light yet warm in tone in order to address the personal and often warm tone of folk art.

investigated alternative materials. Through his research we selected a type of white bronze called Tombasil that has all the appropriate properties. It is reflective, warm in colour and has been used for firehouse nozzles, propeller fittings and tombstone lettering. Thus, it has excellent strength and weathering characteristics. Its high copper content of 57% makes it an expensive metal costing about $1.20 per pound. Our fabrication costs are relatively low however because we are casting the material in the Tallix Foundry in Beacon, New York, in an open cast method (heating the material to 2000 degrees and pouring it directly onto a concrete or steel plate to cool). The resulting pour receives the imperfections of the surface on which it was cast.

A steel surface produces a flatter finish, showing the liquid flow of the metal and a concrete surface produces a cratered and coarse finish.

Once all panels were cast, they were assembled and set on the facade and the intention to create a structure that is at once ordinary and extraordinary seemed intact. We were surprised and nervous as the first panels went up because they were more varied in colour and darker than we had expected. Later, as the last panels were put into place, literally hours before the museum opening, we found that we were pleased with the darker quality of the metal. The natural patina produced a moodiness that changed with the particular light conditions of the time of day and the weather. The colour ranges from a warm amber to a rather sombre and flat dark-brown. MAFA's facade, in the tradition of architecture and construction, produces an original facade pertinent to the museum's desires, the programme and the context. On budget and capable of withstanding the elements, there is little doubt it will perform. Although unique in its material and composition, the facade is about the limits of its formal properties and performance. It is very much about centring.

The development of the MAFA facade and our experiments at Tallix have stimulated our curiosity. Tallix has also rediscovered new ways to use traditional materials and casting methods. They too are excited and curious about the possibilities of the material and about exploring new ways to use the foundry. Recent 'play' at Tallix has allowed us to extend our limits. ◪

Tod Williams, Billie Tsien & Associates, Museum of American Folk Art, New York, 2002

Above
The casting sequence of the Tombasil panels at the Tallix Foundry and a mock-up assembly of the external wall helped in developing an understanding of the properties and quality of the material.

After considering site-cast concrete and realising that it is more absorbent than reflective and also impractical to cast in midtown Manhattan, we turned to aluminium.

The cast aluminium was dull in finish and not warm in colour. Matt Baird, our project architect,

Billie Tsien received a BFA from Yale University in 1971 and an M.Arch from UCLA in 1977. From 1971 to 1975 she was a painter and teacher. She has taught at SCI-Arc, Yale, Harvard GSD, the University of Texas at Austin and the University of Michigan. She has worked with Tod Williams since 1977, and they have been in partnership since 1986.

Tod Williams received his undergraduate degree from Princeton University in 1965. He read architecture at Cambridge in 1966 and received MFA and M.Arch degrees from Princeton in 1967. He taught at the Copper Union from 1974 to 1989 and has held visiting professorships at a number of schools of architecture since the mid-1980s. In 1982 he received an Advanced Fellowship from the American Academy in Rome.

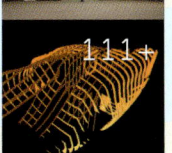

Outside

The Westin New York hotel tower, on 43rd Street in Times Square, is that rare example of a holistic high-rise built recently in Manhattan. From the ground up, it is almost entirely the vision of a single design firm. **Craig Kellogg** looks at the total building to see how its architects have blurred the line between interiors and exteriors to realise a complete, if controversial, aesthetic vision.

In

Previous page
Behind the long, linear check-in desk at the Westin New York
Hotel, a hotel by Arquitectonica, is a wood-panelled wall that
features fractured planes similar to those of the exterior facade.

Below
The elevator core, which is treated as an object within
the generous open-plan lobby, has been wrapped in
vertical glass strips back-painted with a metallic frit.

'It is both shrill and banal,' critic Paul Goldberger wrote not
long ago in the *New Yorker* magazine, 'less a piece of
architecture than a developer's box in drag. The Westin forces
you, as no piece of architecture in this city has in a very long
time, to come to terms with exactly what makes a building so
strident that it enthralls in the way a gruesome accident does.'
From a Manhattan architecture critic, these are strong words
indeed. Nevertheless, Goldberger also praises the project. He
notes the 'splendid' punched metal wall-panels inside the
elevator cabs. And upstairs, at the back of the structure, is a
seven-storey interior atrium, wallpapered with the same
reflective glass as the curtain wall outside and slashed by the
same glowing curved line that crosses the exterior facade.
Goldberger finds the effect in the atrium 'completely engaging'.

Towers built today in New York are mostly collaborations
between various architects and designers, where each party is
responsible for different elements. But Arquitectonica, the
Miami firm that designed the facade of the Westin, also created
the lobbies, bar, guest rooms and even custom furniture and
area rugs. Arquitectonica principals Laurinda Spear and
Bernardo Fort-Brescia are by no means new to interiors. Spear
created a range of popular wallpapers for the adventurous
American manufacturer Wolf-Gordon. Some of her patterns,
Spear told me at the time, were inspired by the graphic
symbols American architects draw on their plans. One of the
most popular was an elaboration of the loopy graphic line
typically used to symbolise wall insulation.

Spear's wonderful patterns are employed in the corridors of
the Westin New York – albeit in soft, earthy colours. It is
surprising to discover, since Times Square is known for being a

loud, tacky neighbourhood of themed restaurants and
tourist shops, that Arquitectonica's interiors for the new
hotel are crisp and fairly chaste. More unexpected still
is the way ideas seen in the facade – elements that have
been trashed by critics like Goldberger – come indoors
so elegantly. Behind the long, lean reception counter, a
crazy quilt of rich wood-grained wall-panels proves
extremely satisfying. Outdoors, the same motif at a
much bigger scale delineates fields of citrus colours,
from blood orange to bark brown, on the enamelled
aluminium portion of the facade. This has given some
critics pause for thought, because at such a large scale
it makes the building feel a little like a cartoon. 'What it
does not look like,' Goldberger wrote, is 'a three-
hundred-and-seventy-million-dollar commercial project
in the center of New York City.'

New York Times critic Herbert Muschamp has
already proposed resurfacing the colourful metal panels
in black and white, with 'some slashes of colour for
accent, perhaps'. He may be right. But indoors, I think
the same colour scheme works well enough since it is a
touch lighter and often frosted or metallic. The elevator
core is wrapped with glass, back-painted in cool,
metallic hues that reference Arquitectonica's Miami
palette. Hard, smooth materials give the space an urban
edge that suits the Manhattan context.

Balcony corridors around the atrium, which lacks
natural illumination since there is no skylight in the
ceiling, offer a vaguely retro kitsch-modern vibe.
Arquitectonica appears to have translated the look from
facades of tropical cast-concrete beachfront resort
hotels of the mid-century, and the effect is heightened
by randomly placed circular lighting fixtures rising like
bubbles across the solid walls of the balcony
balustrades.

Unlike facades, interiors such as these are
designed to survive inspection at close range. By
contrast there is no question that the exterior
envelope of the Westin lacks fine detail. The curtain
wall looks cheap – and it probably was. Few
Manhattan developers decide to lavish unnecessary
sums on elegant window systems for high-rises when
they can get away with spending less.

But, looking at the facade and massing, the *New
Yorker* magazine asks, 'Is this the ugliest building in
New York?' My answer is no. The developer chose an
architect, not a committee, to design his hotel. So the
Westin is more than its shell. Unlike much that passes
for architecture today, it is a fully realised concept, not
just a decorated shed thrust into the sky. A building with
interiors as good as these is not simply an ugly building.
At the very least, Arquitectonica should be praised for
pushing to make the Westin strong and complete, an
architectural whole that is the sum of all of its parts. ⌂

Below
A reflective wall treatment in the indoor atrium of the Westin New
York utilises the curtain-wall glazing system from the facade.
Round light fixtures are sprayed like bubbles across the balustrades
of corridors that ring the void.

Below
The gridshell structure uses minimal materials to achieve a large enclosure.
Each structural component is stressed by double curvature to bring it to
its maximum potential and, acting compositely with the other components,
assumes a single structural form. The green oak used at the Weald and
Downland Museum is especially environmentally friendly, coming from a
sustainable source, self-finished and itself embodying far smaller amounts
of energy than manufactured materials.

Downland Gridshell
at the Weald and Downland
Open Air Museum, Chichester

For its new conservation and visitor centre, the Weald and Downland Open Air Museum in Sussex, a museum that on site has one of the finest collections of medieval timber buildings, required 'a structure that caught the essence of timber construction and threw it forward into the third millennium'. **Jeremy Melvin** describes how Edward Cullinan Architects and engineers Buro Happold met this criterion with their development of the gridshell, a building form that has its origins in Second World War timber aircraft construction.

To see skilled carpenters working on old timbers in the new gridshell at the Weald and Downland Open Air Museum is to enjoy an extraordinary opportunity to appreciate the true significance and potential of timber construction. It is as if the flowing, swelling and twisting new form is a perfect contemporary analogue for the meaning, significance and innovation with which medieval carpenters imbued their work. The space is like three pulses with two points of constriction, suggesting yet not demanding a division into units, and the long timber laths add perspective to their curving effects, their slenderness belying the overall strength of the form. It is in this space that relics acquired by the museum come to be preserved before re-erection outside, where students can study conservation techniques and visitors see the efforts that go into the results they can enjoy across the museum's estate in the Sussex village of Singleton. There can be few better confluences of the preservation and education remits of any museum.

But, says museum director Richard Harris, it is wrong to assume that the innovative timber gridshell technique developed here by Edward Cullinan Architects and engineers Buro Happold has exactly the same role in contemporary society as that of advanced carpentry in the Middle Ages. Referring to the tie-beam lap dovetail joint, an encapsulation

of the ethos of traditional timber construction, Harris says 'it was part of a culturally defined system, part of a universally accepted system of doing buildings', where the gridshell is 'a wonderful invention'. The correspondence between them comes instead in the way that 'you can read what the structure is telling you about the space you occupy – structure has an impact on space', or put another way, that synthesis of form and function is what architecture is all about. This interaction between two separate cultural programmes has a piquant and not totally unrelated parallel in the way that eccentric millionaire Edward James invited Salvador Dalí to lend surrealism to the interior of his Lutyens-designed house, notably with the famous 'lips' sofa. The house, West Dean Park, is adjacent to the museum's property and it was James who donated the land in 1971. In both cases the contrast between two totally different ways of looking at the world helps to reveal more about both than either would alone.

The story of the gridshell has that curious retrospective inevitability that great projects often have, though it must have seemed anything but inevitable to the museum, Cullinans and Happolds

Top
As the gridshell was lowered from a horizontal position about 7 metres above the slab, it assumed the form analysis showed it would take, picking up the serpentine cantilevers off the concrete floor slab above the semi-basement artefact store.

Bottom
Below the gridshell, in a concrete box, is a semi-basement artefact store. Its location and materials make it ideal for the environmentally controlled storage and security conditions that museums have to meet, but the design also uses the thermal mass of the ground to moderate the temperature bank fresh air entering the workshop.

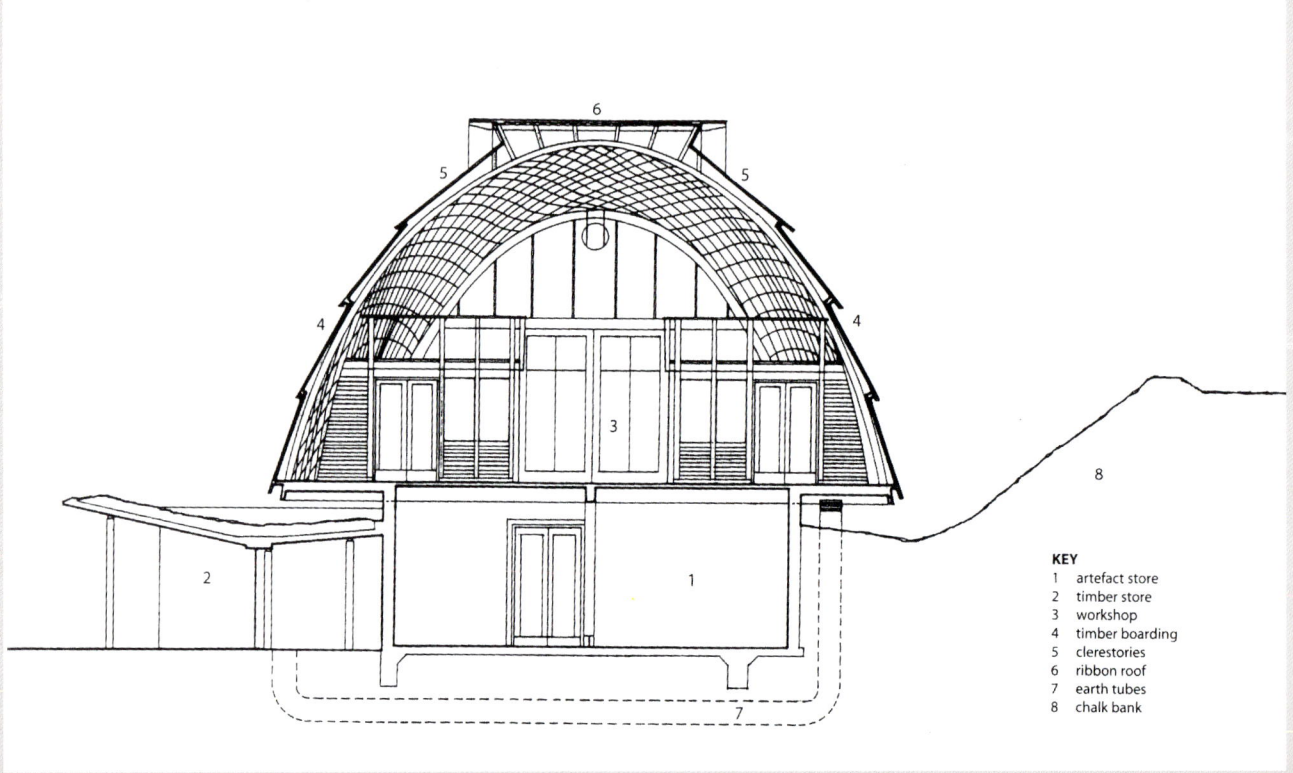

KEY
1 artefact store
2 timber store
3 workshop
4 timber boarding
5 clerestories
6 ribbon roof
7 earth tubes
8 chalk bank

during its long gestation from 1995 until the building's completion in 2002. Simultaneously with outgrowing workshop facilities it had leased from a nearby farmer, the museum recognised the potential of the National Lottery to fund a major new project that might have plenty of space for teaching, watching and conservation, as well as a modern, environmentally controlled artefact store. Maybe if Westminster Hall had become surplus to parliamentary requirements there would have been a genuine medieval timber-framed building of adequate size, but most such buildings, certainly those possessed by the museum, are domestic or agricultural in scale. A new building presented the choice of an overblown pastiche that would have negated the careful authenticity with which the genuine artefacts are presented, or a structure that caught the essence of timber construction and threw it forward into the third millennium. It was also more congenial to the Heritage Lottery Fund and the various private trusts that provided finance.

Cullinans and Happolds have done an enormous amount to expand the repertoire of timber construction. As Cullinans' Robin Nicholson points out, using locally sourced timbers the process uses a tiny proportion of embodied energy compared to almost any other form of construction, but it also has extraordinary architectural possibilities. Ted Cullinan once drew a cartoon of an archer and someone tossing the caber to

illustrate its extremes, and his designs have explored both. Numerous innovative timber projects have emanated from Buro Happold, including several at Hooke Park with Cullinans and Ahrends, Burton and Koralek, but most notably the Mannheim Garden Festival structure of 1975, which Ted Happold designed with Frei Otto shortly before Ted left Arup. Michael Dickson, who took over the chairmanship of Buro Happold when its founder died, had contributed to that project, and with the Weald and Downland Museum recognised the opportunity he had long sought to do another.

A gridshell is essentially a way of achieving a long span with thin, pliable strips laid out flat and then raised or lowered into its self-determining double curvature form. The principle is fairly simple and has its origins in Second World War timber aircraft but, especially on the scale of a building, the contingent difficulties multiply rapidly. Until relatively recently the only way of establishing the form the gridshell would take was to build models; even now physical models are used in design development alongside computers. It is a structure that begs for timber – although the Japanese architect Shigeru Ban used cardboard tubes at the Hanover Expo 2000 – and the Singleton gridshell uses two layers of green oak

Top
Lowering the gridshell from the level plane on which it was assembled took nine days.

Bottom
From the outset the concept was for a woodworking facility in a woodland setting.

laths. But timber does not grow in suitable lengths without becoming too thick to tense and bend, and as the entire concept depends on the timbers straining against each other to make them act in concert, the structure demands innovative connections.

Given that the building is almost 50 metres long, between 16 and 11 metres wide and 10 metres high at its tallest point, the timbers themselves had to be joined with finger and scarf joints into lengths of about 35 metres for the arched members and even longer for the horizontal sheer members. The arches run diagonally across the space, the two layers interweaving with each other to make the gridshell. Where they meet are specially designed node clamps, a deceptively simple series of three plates that hold the inner layer of each member closely in position while allowing the outer layer to move as the grid began to assume its final form. Away from the nodes the two layers are kept apart with sheer blocks that ensure they act compositely. Above is a layer of insulation and, apart from two strips of polycarbonate rooflights either side of the apex, the cladding is timber.

Construction was an unusual blend of empirical experimentation and theoretical conception. The Green Oak Carpentry Company joined the team at an early stage to bring their expertise to bear, while Cullinans and Happolds gradually determined the shell's form with models and computers. Robin Nicholson remembers how one model showed that the proposed half-metre gap between laths was necessary only in the valleys, emphasising the constriction of the space by adding more lines at the point where others converge. An advance on the four timber gridshells used previously was to build this one in the air on movable props and a sacrificial layer of plywood. Slowly lowering the props over nine days meant the shell assumed its form with gravity rather than being forced upwards, allowing it to be monitored more accurately and causing less damage. As it lowered it slowly picked up the serpentine form of the floor, cantilevered from the concrete-box artefact store in the semi-basement below.

It is a magnificent space, combining grandeur with the comforting tactility of timber, the craft of carpentry with innovative construction. It may be, as Richard Harris puts it, a 'wonderful invention', but it joins a small group of gridshell structures, and one which will grow if Cullinans have their way. They are already proposing similar forms for the Cambridge Botanical Garden, and Nicholson has also cited its suitability for one-off single-volume structures such as sports halls. ∆

Below
**Camera obscura, planned for a second phase of construction in Mitchell Park,
Greenport, New York, due for completion in 2003**
Architects: Sharples Holden Pasquarelli (SHoP). Engineers: Buro Happold.
Extract from construction drawings generated from digital solid model of project.
Digital modelling enabled design of complexly formed components to fit the
unconventional building form. Manipulation of the information in the model also
allowed subsequent presentation for fabrication of the components (via digital
files for CNC or templates for manual cutting, depending on the contractors'
capabilities) as well as creation of step-by-step assembly instructions through
selective display of successive component sets. Contractor confidence is
improved and construction cost lowered as a consequence.

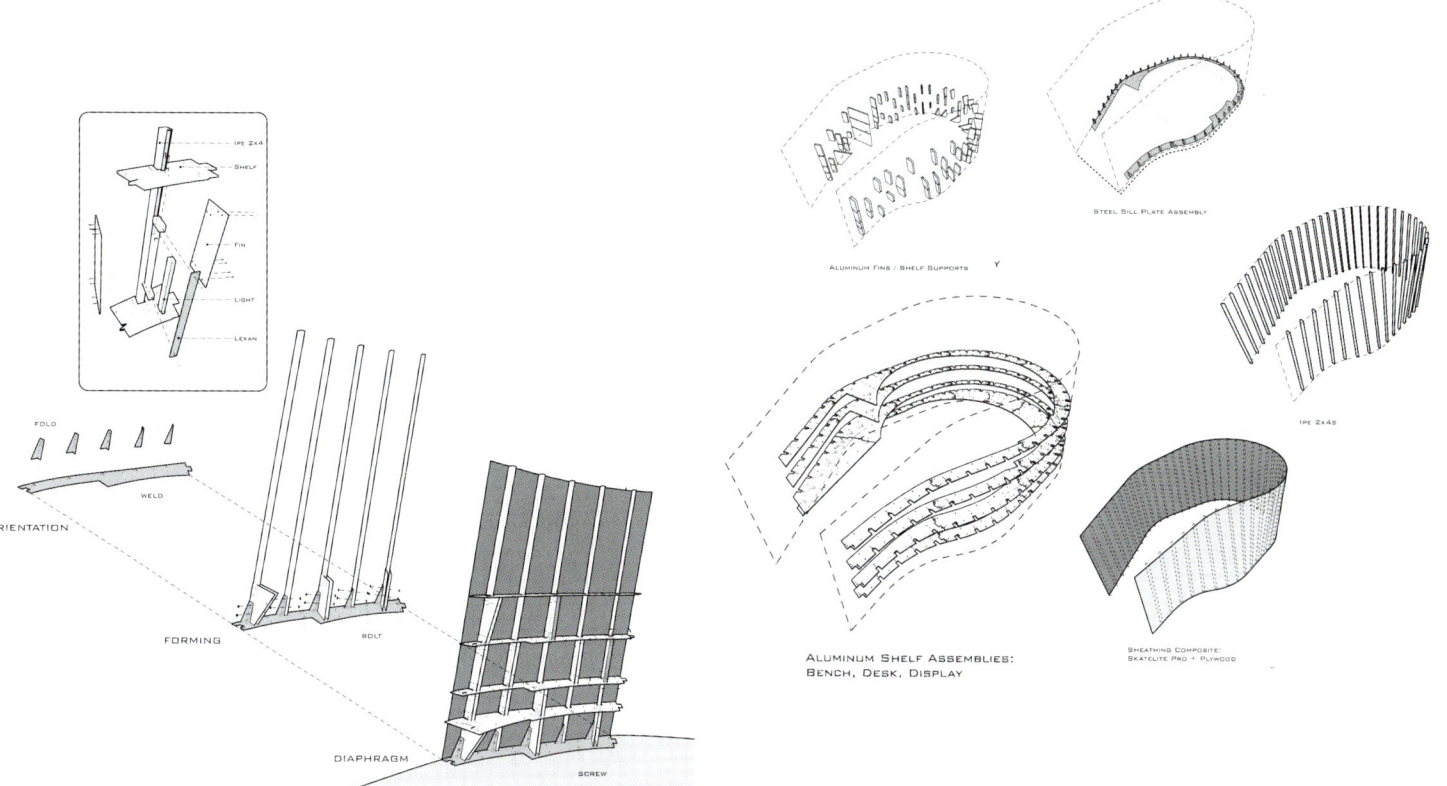

Blurring the Lines

An Exploration of Current CAD/CAM Techniques

Computer-aided design and manufacturing are relatively well-established
practices in the aeronautics/aerospace, automotive and shipbuilding industries.
But although these practices have elicited much interest in recent years
within the building industry and the allied fields of architecture and building
engineering, their application here is as yet in a nascent state. At present
there is (fortunately) no widespread agreement as to how, or indeed even why,
CAD/CAM should be employed in designing and fabricating the built environment.
This is the first of a series of 'Engineering Exegesis' articles, edited by **André
Chaszar**, in this volume of D that will aim to survey some of the areas of
current development in CAD/CAM for buildings and highlight the critical questions
and assumptions underlying them. Though 'blurring the lines' may seem a
strange phrase to associate with digital tools the underlying premise of which
is precision, we will see that the communicative and cognitive opportunities
they offer break down many of the distinctions now entrenched in building.

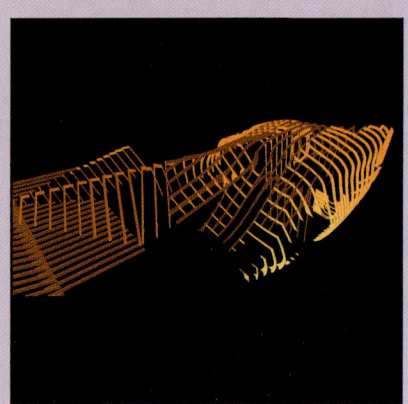

Most architects and engineers have by now accepted the role of CAD as a drafting aid, and to some extent it is now seen as obligatory even on projects where it is not necessarily useful. But those at the forefront of CAD use have recognised more extensive capabilities, and the potential of CAM for building is now beginning to be explored. In what follows, the emphasis will perforce be on design aimed at the construction of buildings, rather than on speculative architecture. Although CAD is proving very useful to 'paper architects' their projects typically sidestep the issues addressed by engineering, not to mention those raised by the M in CAM.

Applications in Other Industries

Considering that CAD/CAM systems were initially developed for applications other than the design and construction of buildings, a useful point of departure for exploring these tools may be to examine what capabilities currently exist in those other fields. Of course, not all of these capabilities are applicable to buildings. Nevertheless, the similarity of these applications in constructional and organisational complexity to that of buildings, as well as their tantalising departure from conventional building forms, makes them a fertile source of ideas. Significant also is the combined wealth of research-and-development efforts found in these fields, in contrast to that in the construction industry.

What are the features of the use of CAD/CAM in these other fields that most inspire architects, building engineers and contractors? In no particular order we might mention:

* *visualisation* – the ability to present graphical information realistically, or otherwise attractively or instructively, to produce physical models aiding comprehension of 3-D forms and to animate 4-D sequences
* *computation* – the ability to perform numerical or even text operations at high speed and with great accuracy, whether for specific solutions or a range of scenarios
* *geometric manipulation* – the ability to deal with forms of great complexity (perhaps hitherto intractable) or relative simplicity, arranging, generating, measuring, modifying and realising them with, again as in computation, improved speed and accuracy
* *standardisation* – the ability to faithfully communicate data from one instance to the next, allowing repetition of a particular design solution in recurring design situations
* *rationalisation* – the ability to make explicit (and thus editable) the decisions leading to particular design solutions, similar to standardisation but actually admitting of great variability.

As suggested by many of the capabilities enumerated above, digital techniques are also useful in a variety of nonmanufacturing areas, such as film making, gaming, and geographic information systems (GIS), some of which have had a significant influence on certain architectural, and to a much lesser extent, engineering practices' design- and particularly presentation methods.

One of the most touted examples of digital techniques is the Boeing 777, which was the first commercially produced airliner to be designed and documented entirely electronically and in 3-D. Along the way, the vast quantity of data and number of participants for the project required the development of numerous new capabilities for data management, rapid visualisation and manipulation of complex graphical files, and concurrent design by widely scattered parties with reliable, frequent updating of changes.

Automotive and industrial design and manufacturing also inspire comparisons to building. Their products are less emphatically objects of utility than boats and aeroplanes – that is, their forms are less constrained by physical performance requirements – and their mass-production (recently recast as 'mass-customisation') techniques enable an enviable degree of economy despite their complexity. On the other hand, their scale is so much smaller and their procurement systems so different that the link is tenuous. Their relevance for us at present

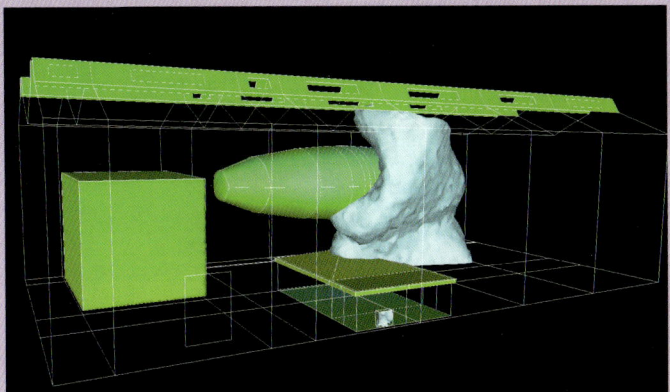 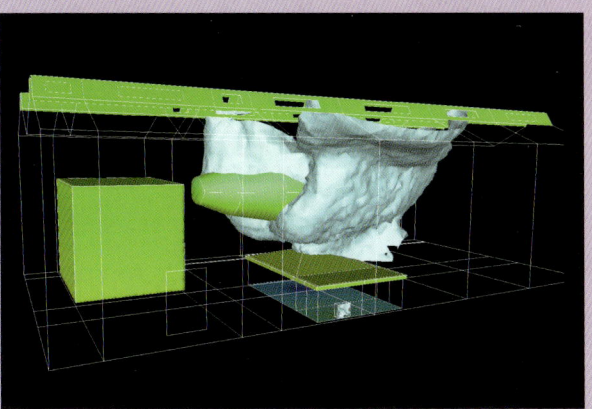

is in certain CAD modelling techniques for 3-D forms and significantly in rapid prototyping, and in certain CAM techniques for components of limited size. The auto industry is also a source of continuing innovations in designer-computer interfaces.

At the moment shipbuilding seems the example most relevant to building design and construction as its products are large and complex yet it has a fragmented procurement system and limited production runs. Many of the strategies being adopted by small boatyards are also highly applicable to buildings, and range from specific layout and forming techniques for curved metal or composite shapes, through designing parts for self-alignment and embedded assembly information to development of customisable 'product models' and re-engineering the entire process from design through commissioning to take best advantage of available CAD/CAM capabilities.[1]

Transferable Technology

To what extent, then, do we believe that the examples of CAD/CAM utilisation in other industries are relevant to architecture and to building? How literally shall we take the idea of 'technology transfer'? As a means of modelling 3-D forms, yes. As a means of checking how these forms fit together, yes. As a means of fabricating components to be assembled into a building, maybe, recognising that many components will not be produced this way. For new tools of project administration, procurement, documentation, collaborative communication, managing file sizes, detail resolution, protocols for information exchange and a host of other minutiae, emphatically yes – let the research resources of mass-production, the military and luxury vehicle industries be leveraged for the benefit of building! At the end of the day what matters most is that the lessons learned in these other applications are used to best advantage and that the claims for the potential of their adoption are not overstated.

Certainly the cognitive process is transferable: new means of construction engender new ways of understanding form, and new means of describing and generating form may do the same. That is, designers can now develop a new 'vocabulary of making' not only for the final product but also for models, documents, etc,

due to a greater variety of tools at hand than there are with traditional drawing/drafting and model making. 'Re-engineering the product' applies not only to the finished building, but potentially to the entire process by which it is conceived, designed, refined and approved for execution – even operated, renovated and dismantled.

On the fabrication and assembly side, some avant-garde architectural practices are seeking manufacturing techniques from other industries which could be applied to building construction. Of particular interest are the smooth, doubly curved forms seen in automotive and aeronautic design, and somewhere near the intersection of deconstruction and radar evasion lies another family of forms gaining the attention of architects. Semi-monocoque rib-and-skin construction systems today find ready translation from airframes and boat hulls to buildings (for example the Lord's Cricket Ground Media Centre), as indeed they already did when, according to some accounts, carpentry first spun off from shipwrighting some millennia ago. The *ne plus ultra* vision of the day is of buildings built by successive milling and deposition of hi-tech, lightweight, super-strong materials by seven-axis CNC machines like those that produce composite-hulled maxi-yachts and the B-2 bomber. Assuming for the moment that this is where we want to go – how do we get there?

Obstacles to successful implementation of these 'transferred technologies' include the lack of familiarity of designers with the specific details of the processes they wish to adapt, insufficient grasp of the general implications of the adapted forms and processes for other, conventionally executed, aspects of the project, and the inability to contract fabricators capable of delivering the speciality product within the customary schedule, budgetary and regulatory constraints of the building construction process.

This is not to suggest that designers must know it all – which most nowadays would agree is impossible –

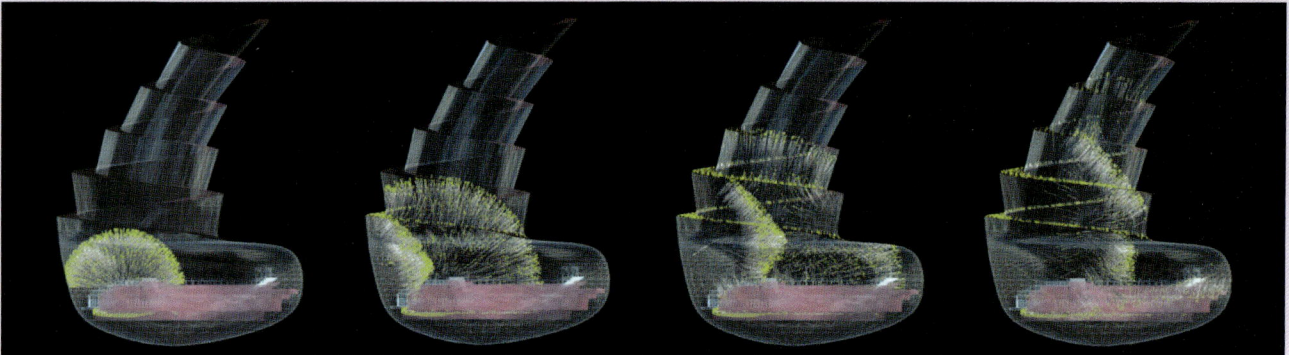

but that they must enlist the cooperation of a variety of specialists to an extent even greater than in conventional construction. Thus, as well as blurring the distinction between design and production (or between 'design intent' and 'means-and-methods') the adoption of digital practices perhaps blurs the lines of authorship. If architects see in this a loss of control, they may find compensation in gaining the ability to specify in greater detail than ever before the form and location of the project's components – that is, to achieve a specific perceptible effect or organisational clarity. The effect on engineers is less clear, as they have always had a reputation for greater interest in tinkering with the physical practicalities of construction. The question remains as yet unanswered: does increasing the use of CAD/CAM result in greater involvement or removal of architectural authorship from the locus of 'making'?

Current CAD/CAM Uses in Building

Beyond the simple electronic drafting and rendering uses noted earlier, where making is restricted to drawings, electronic files and the odd stereolithograph, more ambitious designers use CAD/CAM for analysis as well as description of building forms. As in the other fields mentioned above, CAD/CAM is used for describing complex forms and/or complex juxtapositions of forms that would be intractable without the capabilities conferred by the software. Transformations of forms are also now enabled, from simple moving, rotating and copying to more sophisticated scaling, stretching and various exotic types of distortions such as shearing, torquing and conforming planar surfaces onto nonplanar surfaces. It can be argued that these operations in and of themselves engender a different cognitive model of form, as well as a different palette of forms than was available to designers accustomed to tools yielding straight lines and circular arcs in drawing or the classic solids – sphere, cube, cone and cylinder – in modelling.

Form-generating tools have become available more recently, giving programmable surfaces and volumes such as radiating, sinusoidally waving surfaces, rescued from captivity in the realm of applied mathematicians' graphing programs to be now at the disposal of any designer interested in the shapes of ripples on water. Other preprogrammed complex mathematical functions, as well as randomised surface disturbances, serve both to enhance renderings and inspire investigation of building forms hitherto unknown. Still more sophisticated algorithms mimic the behaviour of paper or fabric by constraining geometry and/or incorporating simulation of physics phenomena. Parametrics and associative geometry on the other hand let designers create customised transformations according to rules that they themselves define, regulating the relationships between specific elements of their digital models.

Even more powerful in the long run are analytical tools that give feedback regarding the forms modelled. Beyond relying on the nearly instinctual visual evaluation process built upon looking at different projected views and renderings, or the somewhat more sophisticated conventions of plans and nonhorizontal sections, designers may now have rapid access to geometric properties of their models such as surface area and enclosed volume, the degree of curvature of nonplanar surfaces and the unfolded shapes of faceted surfaces. Analysis of geometric properties such as curvature are of particular importance in assessing the constructibility of complex shapes, for which the choice of material and fabrication process are more explicitly critical than for planar and orthogonal forms.

Still somewhat distinct from CAD/CAM proper but slowly becoming more closely integrated are engineering analysis programs such as those employed for quantitative assessment of structural, HVAC (heating, ventilation and air conditioning), acoustical and lighting designs. Engineering procedures were encoded digitally in archaic languages well before the advent of the first CAD system or computer numerically controlled (CNC) cutter, in order to execute numerical calculations more rapidly and accurately. As these programs become more sophisticated, so they tend to incorporate greater measures of graphical input and output to supplement lines of code and tables of results (even to the extent that at times, unfortunately, the changes are solely graphical, with the underlying engineering code unreviewed and unimproved). In this process, engineering programs are becoming more CAD-like, though at the moment it seems that these developments from opposing shores risk missing each other mid-chasm, like the apocryphal mis-surveyed bridge. Another exciting area of progress is in modelling of construction logistics, such as time-lapse construction sequence models for studying the suitability of delivery schedules and erection procedures.

Opportunities in CAD/CAM for Buildings

In addition to extending our capabilities for formal invention and analysis, as described above, some other important opportunities arise as we delve further into the potentials of CAD/CAM in building, addressing some of our previous quandaries and inevitably raising new ones.

As collaborative tools, CAD and CAM both surpass most, if not all, previous means for quickly and accurately sharing ideas and information. Once hurdles of file-format compatibility and interoperability in general are better addressed, architects, engineers and contractors will be much better able to advance the process of design within ever tighter timetables, perhaps even eliminating an entire caste of project managers in consequence. The quality of design will also improve on various fronts, from relatively mundane coordination- and interference-checking issues to more thoroughly refined and integrated designs resulting from quicker feedback and more sophisticated analysis. Design models may be developed that simultaneously provide information about formal and performance effects of design moves, for example by recalculating the dimensions of structural elements in response to changing the building form and allowing immediate discussion of this between architects and engineers. Similarly, design models linked to CAM processes could keep close track of fabrication quantity, time and cost effects. In fact at some point the challenge becomes to intelligently limit the type and amount of feedback so as to avoid distraction.

Closely related but distinct from collaboration is the opportunity for vertical integration of various stages in the process from conceptual design through to fabrication, and possibly even erection and operation of the building, as noted earlier. Notwithstanding the impossibility (and undesirability) of creating 'universal design tools', the impulse is in some cases valid to make, for example, a software suite that can be used from sketching ideas to cutting fabric, as in programs developed some years ago for use on tensile structures. Currently available software can also be used from framing layout and structural calculation phases to detailing and making bills of material for standard steel-framed construction. More general tools would again be useful to help designers assess feasibility, even at the early stages of a project, especially vis-à-vis complex forms.

Of course the obverse of potentials are limitations, and the question arises: What may be the effects of the choice of digital tools on the resulting architecture? Designers using computers face an array of technical choices and must develop ways of working around and exploiting the quirks of various tools, and

software in particular. The range of choices and their effects far exceeds the consequences of the quandaries of earlier generations: pen or pencil, vellum or mylar, T-square or parallel rule?

Within particular software, for example, choices of smooth versus faceted modelling have implications for file sizes, rendering (or even simple view rotation) time required, the types of manipulations to which the model's elements may be subjected and finally the efficacy with which model data is translated to machine paths. No one set of tools does it all, and most designers find themselves relying on a collection selected on the basis of familiarity, cost and demonstrated results, which leaves some trace on the design work alongside the designers' own. As always, one mark of mastery is the extent to which designers can bend the tools to their will.

Given the number of producers and types of end users we may posit that rather than converging, some tools will remain most suitable for conceptual design and presentation (for example as 'digital sketching', renderings and animations for clients) and others will be required to make the leap into producing information suitable for the construction of buildings. Interfaces among these will be one of the key areas of development, and to the extent that designers have a stake in how they function designers should also make an effort to influence their programming.

Future Tools and Uses

Given the possibilities already indicated, what would we like to be able to do with CAD/CAM, and what new capabilities are currently in development?

One of the more intriguing directions being explored by some architects (such as G Lynn, B Cache/Objectile, SHoP, SU-11 and Kol/Mac) is mass-customisation for buildings. In these scenarios basic building shells or frames are outfitted – inside, outside or both – with elements chosen by their prospective occupants. These may be along the lines of built-in furniture and fixtures, or larger elements such as additional rooms, alcoves, mezzanines, penthouses and so forth. The basic shell or frame may also be modifiable within some parameters. This kind of design concept is aided by CAD tools like the various distortions mentioned but even more powerfully by parametric modelling and associative geometry capabilities. When linked to engineering analysis and a construction system that is equally malleable, standardised but tailored buildings may finally be realised after decades of experimentation. Malleable building models would also be able to respond with some sophistication to varying site conditions or other external constraints upon their form (for example environmental factors, sightlines and zoning envelopes).

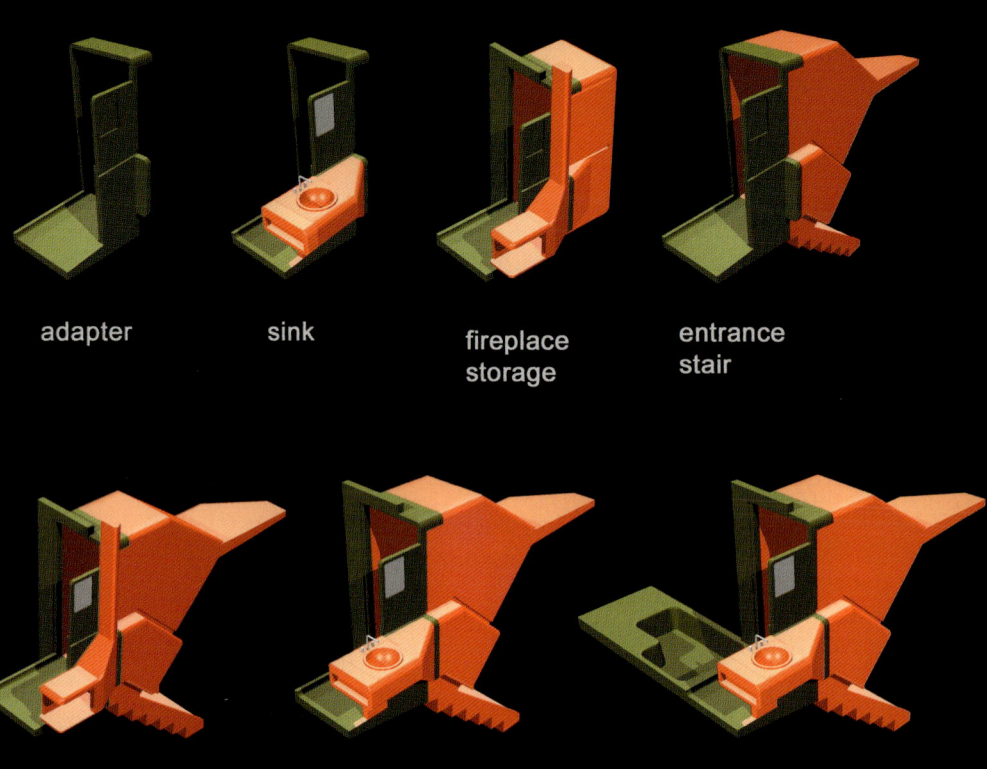

Add-On Variations

adapter   sink   fireplace storage   entrance stair

Carried through to the level of construction detailing and linked to some degree of CAM-based fabrication, the variations called for may eventually be realisable economically as well.

Another important area of development – more prosaic but perhaps of more imminent impact – is in the use of building models for facilities management. Features of this range from a comprehensive building database (product model) encompassing all of the building's fixed and moveable components, complete with bills of quantity, certificates, warranties, and maintenance or operating manuals – all generated essentially as part of the design and construction documentation – to real-time monitoring and control of lighting, air, heating and cooling and other environmental systems, as well as tracking of energy consumption, equipment replacement and building renovations to fine-tune the building's operation based on actual patterns of use. Given access to this feedback, designers could better evaluate opportunities for improving their projects (or re-engineering their products).

Looking into the more distant future, we may see artificial intelligence being brought into CAD/CAM. With artificial intelligence we can imagine the incorporation of 'expert systems' to aid designers at various stages in their work, and in CAM we may eventually see manufacturing processes that learn during fabrication of a series of components, optimising not only

shape nesting or cutting paths but even redesigning elements based on this information for consideration by the designers. The editorial variety of design activity would then move beyond selecting from a field of forms rule-generated in CAD to selecting from forms refined by the internal analysis of the fabrication apparatus. We could designate this CGD/CGM – computer-generated design/manufacturing – if we dare let our machines run on so long a leash.

A number of other significant questions also emerge, such as the following.

Will CAM eventually be able to produce fully 3-D forms in building-scale elements (rather than the hardware scale of today) or will complex forms continue to be made from 2-D elements assembled into 3-D aggregates? This depends to some extent on the types of materials available and the degree of pressure to reduce quantities and weight in building (where it is not so critical as in vehicle design). Important too will be developments in fabrication techniques: bending vs forming of metal, glass or plastic sheets, laser sintering, milled vs adjustable formwork, casting of various material and so on.

Should designers be programmers (and vice versa)?

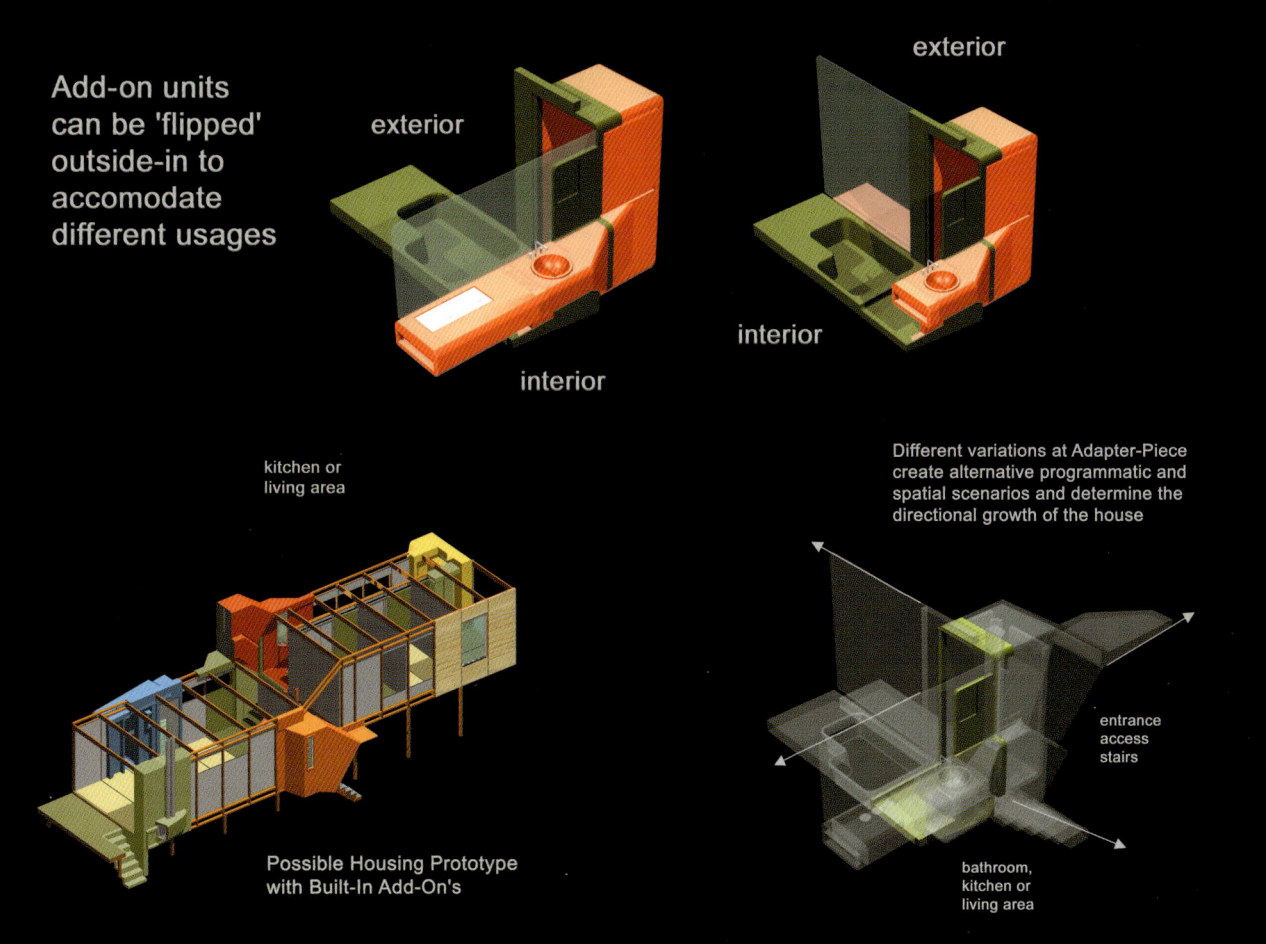

Add-on units can be 'flipped' outside-in to accomodate different usages

exterior

interior

exterior

interior

kitchen or living area

Different variations at Adapter-Piece create alternative programmatic and spatial scenarios and determine the directional growth of the house

entrance access stairs

Possible Housing Prototype with Built-In Add-On's

bathroom, kitchen or living area

Some architects and likely more engineers have a cognitive predisposition to designing in this way. However, some observers claim that programmers can more easily become designers than the other way around. Certainly the rationality of computing and the irrationality or intuition of much good design work become more intricately intertwined with the growing use of cad/cam. And the extent to which architecture realised in building can remain an artistic endeavour will depend to a large extent on the ability of the building industry to continue to attract people so gifted.

To what extent does CAD/CAM promote or inhibit collaboration, especially across disciplines? In its ability to streamline communication and its tendency to elicit earlier input from more specialists, as discussed above, it does seem to promote collaboration. On the other hand, the potential programmer/nonprogrammer schism may worsen these prospects.

And will digital techniques become the only means of designing (not to speak of building)? Well, not in the foreseeable future, judging by the generally acclaimed example of Gehry Partners and others with successful hybrid design methods. Although many young designers claim that the use of computers comes more naturally to them than sketching or model building by hand, it seems that the most intelligent practice is to recognise the complementarity of various tools,

digital or otherwise, and apply them intermixedly as needs and intuition suggest. Furthermore, it is likely to take quite some time until even a majority of those operations that obviously would benefit from being computerised become so. Until then, the tension between digital and nondigital practices is sure to bring with it its share of frustration and inspiration. ∆

Note
1. See the excellent article by C Barry *et al*, 'Keys to CAD/CAM in small shipyards', The Society of Naval Architects and Marine Engineers (Jersey City, NJ) for an illuminating discussion of critical issues in applying CAD/CAM to existing industrial practices.

The next article in the series, written by Mark Burry, will deal more specifically with CAD, exploring among other things visualisation tools, parametrics, associative geometry and how CAD aids the designer in analysis as well as invention.

André Chaszar is the author of this article and the editor of the 'Blurring the Lines' series. An engineer, who is currently on sabbatical from Buro Happold, he is pursuing research in CAD/CAM while teaching and working in independent practice.

Below
The Cohen Compound is the guesthouse Toshiko Mori designed for a house by Paul Rudolph in Casey Key, Sarasota, Florida

James Carpenter Design Associates

+

Toshiko Mori Architect

James Carpenter started out studying architecture at the Rhode Island School of Design and became an artist. Toshiko Mori started out studying art at the Cooper Union and became an architect. Their paths crossed. They married. Now, more than 20 years later, they work in adjacent but separate offices on the same floor of a loft building popular with architects in Lower Manhattan – when they are in town. He travels around the world to oversee projects. She chairs the department of architecture at the Harvard Graduate School of Design. Both break boundaries and occasionally they do work together, expanding the palette of architectural materials. **Jayne Merkel** describes the work of an artist who operates on an architectural scale and an architect with an artist's sensibility on the edges of what are now mainstream architectural concerns.

James Carpenter

In one sense, James Carpenter has come full circle. The work space of James Carpenter Design Associates looks more like an architect's office than an artist's studio. Half a dozen people are working at desks in a neat, airy, high-ceilinged room with models and building materials propped here and there. Most of them were trained as architects. Carpenter works on buildings with teams of architects and engineers instead of alone on freestanding objects, and often solves problems posed by a structure already in design, instead of inventing problems himself. But his main concern, 'perception', is that of an artist. As a student, he was drawn to a particular material – glass – and worked with the well-known glass artist Dale Chihuly, who was teaching at the Rhode Island School of Design at the time. However, unlike most students of the medium, it was not the craft that appealed to Carpenter, but the way glass affects what you see, 'how light informs the experience of a particular site'. Glass can be tinted, bent, frosted or handled in dozens of ways. Each one changes what you see. It can be transparent or reflective like a mirror, present or absent.

Carpenter describes his early work as concerned with 'how information is captured in materials'. After graduation he worked at Corning, where the head of the Corning Museum, Tom Bichner, was exploring the potential of glass. During his time off, Carpenter made films and film installations to show how it is possible to see through glass, or water, and notice reflections on the surface at the same time. Film, with its time sequences, helped illustrate how you tend to see through the surface first and notice it only later or under unusual conditions, like those that exist when very intense direct light is reflected. The films, like architecture, were intended to define space. Carpenter wants to draw attention to the glass and its effect, to focus on awareness of the information that is edited out – or taken in unconsciously.

He also learned a lot from engineers who were testing the properties of materials in ways architects and artists rarely did. At the time, he points out, glass did not have a presence, a literature, the way other materials did. Interest in glass, which has a very ancient history, resurfaced in the 19th century during the Arts and Crafts Movement and in forward-looking structures like the Crystal Palace, for which, he notes, every piece of glass was hand blown. 'The Crystal Palace pushed the limits of the size of a pane that could be made by hand', he says. 'Because glass was treated as an abstraction, industrial advances in producing ever larger pieces of glass were not particularly noticed.'

Carpenter is fascinated by the interaction of glass with light: 'On metal, all you see are reflections. On glass you have reflections but you can also see what is on the other side. Light carries the information. Glass embodies the light'. This idea is potently illustrated in the facade of the German Foreign Ministry in Berlin, designed with Müller Reimann Architects with Schlaich Bergermann & Partners, engineers, and completed in 1999. The Lichthof facade, which looks out over a historic square, has been designed to form 'an important boundary through which the public views the Foreign Office, the civil servants view the city, and in which the images of both sides are reflected'.

Sometimes Carpenter and his colleagues record the behaviour of light without even using glass. At the entrance to the 2000 Olympic Park in Sydney, Australia, they collaborated with Hargreaves Associates landscape architects in the design of a row of 90-foot-tall steel masts that rise out of a mangrove stream. Cruciform-

shaped, polished stainless-steel fins at the top of the masts had misting nozzles in the corners to create a band of mist across the stream. Another mast half a mile away held a grid of mirrored dichroic glass (coated with two colours) that tracked the sun and projected a beam through the mist.

Working with Richard Meier and Thomas Phifer in the late 1990s on the glass 'lens ceiling' of the special proceedings courtroom at Richard Meier & Partners' Federal Building and US Courthouse in Phoenix, Carpenter designed a series of convex discs that reflect a mirror image of the ceiling on the floor. The discs, which are held in place by a suspended cable net structure, diffuse artificial light while clear glass around the perimeter lets in natural light from the ceiling of the atrium and offers glimpses of the sky from inside the courtroom. His work here, as in other places, was funded by a Percent for Art programme.

In Bonn, Carpenter has designed a patterned triangular stair tower for Murphy Jahn's new Deutsche Post headquarters. The building, which faces the Rhine, consists of two volumes: a 240-metre office tower and a three-storey base with a gridded shell roof. The moirè stair tower in the base carries pedestrians to and from the river and acts as an orientation marker. It is clad with patterned laminated glass panels, which look like a grid of small mirrors on a blue field from the inside and a grid of blue rectangles on a reflective field from the outside. The dematerialising pattern contrasts intriguingly with the strong triangular shape of the stair tower itself. Two glass viewing balconies – one facing the tower, the other facing the river – and the stair tower itself will be illuminated at night.

At the Tulane University Student Center in New Orleans, Louisiana, Carpenter and his associates are helping Vincent James add a 60,000-square-foot extension to a 112,000-square-foot structure built in 1959. An enormous new pavilion, with a glass roof supported on piloti, will create a series of outdoor and semi-enclosed spaces, envelop much of the existing building, reorient the centre within the campus precinct, facilitate pedestrian circulation and improve the appearance of the centre. Taking advantage of the warm climate, the scheme provides a new covered porch next to a campus quadrangle and roofs over part of a pocket park, which will have easy access to a popular coffee shop, a food court and an enlarged book store.

To counter the humidity in Louisiana, shade will be provided by a perforated roof and aluminium bifold shutters on the western and southern facades; ceiling fans will circulate air; and a blue wall with chilled water will remove vapour from the air. Some of these ideas were inspired by historic buildings in New Orleans' French Quarter. Most of these devices simply provide shade and move the air. The design of the perforated metal roof, however, is a little more complicated. 'It is being designed to prevent thermal gain but will be sufficiently transparent to allow views of the sky,' Carpenter explains. His involvement here is more comprehensive than in most of his other projects.

Long-term histories of collaboration like that between Carpenter and Vincent James enable Carpenter's group to play a more active role in the early stages of design and explore light, reflection and transparency using different materials in an integral way. None of these collaborations, of course, is quite like that with Toshiko Mori. Though their influence on one another is usually indirect and casual, from time to time they work together, as in the design of Issey Miyake's Pleats Please in New York's SoHo and on the Silverstein House in Florida.

Below
Issey Miyake Boutique
The shop at the corner of Madison Avenue and 77th Street opened before
a whole cluster of international retail outlets moved into the
neighbourhood and before a Minimalist aesthetic became *de rigueur*
for high-fashion shops. But Toshiko Mori's delicate touch and bold,
innovative use of structural fibreglass, like her quiet restraint, parallel
the designer's own approach and sensibility.

Toshiko Mori

From the beginning, Toshiko Mori's research, practice and teaching have been intertwined. Her first professional job grew out of her thesis at the Cooper Union – a 1000-square-foot prototype for a retail display. Almost naively, she took it to Henri Bendel, the luxury clothing store known for cutting-edge design at the time. The people there asked her to adapt it to their Issey Miyake shop. The thesis project also helped her develop expertise in site-specific installation, which she went on to use in shops and museum exhibitions where she has experimented with materials rarely used in architecture. In the Issey Miyake boutique at Bendel's, she riveted structural fibreglass lumacite panels to very thin stainless-steel bars, giving them lateral stability. According to Mori: 'This interest in economy of means came from my Japanese background and my natural frugality'.

In 1987, Issey Miyake invited her to design a store at 77th Street and Madison Avenue. Echoing the designer's use of very light, efficient polyester in his clothing, she used structural fibreglass, again, as a lateral brace for a thin stainless-steel frame and to support the gridded box for cubicles, panels for stair railings and for the changing booths. For Mori, the delicacy and fragility of fibreglass challenges the masculine aesthetic of heaviness – the 'femininisation of aesthetics and technology'.

Ten years later, she designed another store for Miyake downtown in a very old building. In order to preserve the shell of the building, which is in the SoHo cast-iron landmark district, and create a suitable environment for the very modern clothing inside, she designed a glass liner for the shop and, collaborating with James Carpenter, covered it with a translucent film that allows clear views in from some angles and blurred images from others, as if the interior was under water.

Most New York architects find themselves working within old buildings in the city, but Mori has been doing so even in the country, and remodelling modern classics. In New Canaan, Connecticut, where modest modern houses are often razed for builders' 'mini mansions', she was asked to renovate a house by John Black Lee, that had been built in 1956 as a prototype, like the case study houses in Los Angeles and experimental homes in Sarasota, Florida. This one had been built out of four-by-fours and wood siding, both of which had rotted. Her 'syntactical displacement' involved replacing the exterior wood columns with two-by-four stainless-steel Ts and extending them to accommodate an 18-inch-tall clerestory for additional height and light. She replaced the existing glass with a new, more substantial stainless-steel window system, which pivots instead of sliding, like that used by James Carpenter and Vincent James at Tulane. She next recycled the old aluminium frames to create a garage. Inside she added stainless steel to the corners of the existing wood columns to make what she describes as 'a bracing system similar to those used to straighten teeth'. She simply cleaned up the old stainless-steel kitchen, which has a new life in a more Miesian pavilion.

The Leaming House now has a Minimalist elegance that is both Japanese and Modernist, like its architect. It was reincarnated eight years ago and still looks new (the stainless-steel columns are simply cleaned with automotive wax every year).

On the coast of Maine, where she and Carpenter spend their rare leisure hours, Mori built a getaway for Nancy Talbot, who founded the clothing chain that carries her name. The idea here was not for Talbot to get away from a city but for her to get away from a busy family compound nearby, so that she can visit with her children

Below left and bottom left
Leaming House, New Canaan, Connecticut
This renovation of a bare-bones 3000-square-foot house, designed by John Black Lee in
1956, preserved the original structure wherever possible and managed to turn it into an
elegant Miesian pavilion with only minimal intervention. Stainless-steel T-shaped columns
replaced rotting wooden four-by-fours on the outside, and inside stainless-steel Ts have
been attached to both sides of the old four-by-fours to reinforce them and support a
clerestory for additional natural light. The major change is in the proportions of the
section and in the colour scheme, where white panels are now grey to blend with the
stainless steel and into the surrounding pine forest.

Below right
Talbot House, North Haven, Maine
A path from a grand old house in a coastal Maine family compound leads to this
easy-to-maintain getaway for a lively grandmother. All on one level, including the
surrounding deck, the house is nestled in tall pines, which are visible through
glass walls and slit-banded windows that provide views from seated positions.

and grandchildren but still have some privacy and entertain friends on her own. The house consists of two rectangles, parallel to one another, with one slightly behind the other, 'straddling an existing path like an umbilical cord', Mori explains. One space is purely for the owner, the other is used for guests. Since her client, who hired a modern interior designer, The Architects Collaborative veteran Mary Kennedy, did not want the house to have a traditional hip roof, Mori invented a pair of roofs that twist around a clerestory. In summer, the clerestory can be opened to allow hot air to escape. In winter, the hot air and black roof-surface help make the snow melt and drip down the channels created by the roof's gentle curves. The west wall is made of commercial shop-window glass; the front and back are faced with 2-inch cedar. Windows are at seating height, and a deck surrounds the house.

At the other end of the East Coast, Mori designed a guesthouse for Paul Rudolph's Burkhardt House, of 1954, on Casey Key, near Sarasota, Florida. Since the clients have three very different grown-up children (a producer, a Chinese scholar and an artist), she built the house in a T-shape to give each one a separate space, stacking the east–west units, and placing an open staircase in the middle. The marine-grade stainless-steel staircase joins them – structurally as a control joint and socially as a gathering place. The staircase landing overlooks the main house 165 feet away. Since the guesthouse is in a hurricane zone and the land is on a sand bar and very unstable, she had to place it on 20-foot pilings and locate habitable space higher than waves crest. While she was at it, she raised it on concrete piloti to the level of the tree tops, where gnarled old oaks offer shade, privacy and beautiful views.

The thermal mass of a concrete roof provides insulation, absorbing heat during the day and giving it off at night. The 3000-square-foot Cohen guesthouse is made of the same exposed brick as Rudolph's original, but the Okala block that Mori used is more pinkish, like a sunset on the horizon. There are open porches and rooms with operable stainless-steel louvre walls, which are set into the stainless-steel columns on the upper floors. Spare, easy-to-maintain furnishings maintain the cool aesthetic and bamboo floors cover poured-in-place horizontal concrete slabs. The ground under the house is covered with crushed shell.

For another client half a mile away, Mori designed a 6000-square-foot house with big open interior spaces. The pilings for the Silverstein House were so expensive that it made sense to place them as far apart as possible and extend them up an additional 8 feet on what is already high ground. The spaces of the house are organised by the horizon. The columns on the perimeter of the Greek temple plan make possible a central staircase, which is hung from the floors above and leads up through a glass floor to a skylit atrium designed by her husband. 'It is as if you are swimming and come up for air,' she explains. Located in a wild tropical landscape, the house has views of the gulf and the bay.

Since local regulations allow construction only where a building already existed, the house occupies the site of a former coastguard station. An abandoned coastguard dormitory has been made into a pool house, and the existing oversized dock has been retained. But the atmosphere now could not be more different. Concrete-block walls set into a concrete frame with 40-feet spacings surround a spacious interior filled with the

Below top

Cohen Compound, Casey Key, Florida
This 3000-square-foot guesthouse for a house designed by Paul Rudolph in the 1950s
perches on a protected sand bar near Sarasota, Florida, with a sea turtle habitat on one
side and a manatee habitat on the other. Though it occupies the footprint of a house
destroyed by a hurricane, piloti raise it around 20 feet above sea level where it enjoys views
of the Gulf of Mexico to the west and Sarasota Bay to the east and is sheltered from storm
surge, flooding, and intense sunlight by live oaks, palms and mangroves. A stainless steel
stair ties together the concrete and Okala block, $1.2 million structure, completed in 1999.
Furnishings were selected for ease of maintenance.

Below bottom

**Toshiko Mori, Surface & Structure, an Installation for an exhibition of Japanese
textiles at the Museum of Modern Art**
Textiles stand, drape, hang and droop in this elegant installation that turned
swathes of fabric into columns, curtains, wall-panels and sculptures. Mori's
pointedly lighted 1999 design emphasised the characteristics of the six categories
the museum used to describe the different kinds of fabrics featured: Transparent,
Dyed, Reflective, Printed, Sculpted and Layered. The galleries were dramatic
enough to make the exhibition a real 'show'.

family's collection of postwar art. The oversized living room is like
a gallery, and the dining room is big enough to accommodate 20
people. Hidden pocket doors adapt the open first-floor plan for
guests. Because light enters from above, the roofs can have wide
protective overhangs. A ramp on one side of the house leads
down to a garden, where there are pebbles underneath the
house, and a wall with a slight blue cast which helps to save
energy. Walking along it feels like being under water.

Mori's sensitivity to colour, light, texture and materials
makes her a particularly attractive candidate for the design of
artists' spaces and exhibition installations. She is converting a
factory in Porterdale, Georgia, into artists' residences, and in
1998 designed the Contemporary Japanese Textiles exhibition
at the Museum of Modern Art (MoMA) in New York. In her
projects, studios and installations she employs materials and
techniques for architectural purposes that were previously
associated with feminine crafts such as cloth making and
weaving. For a refugee shelter, she used polar fleece and
Goretex donated by Patagonia. At MoMA she draped textiles
over a stainless-steel cable system from Arakawa Hardware.
She suspended thinner fabrics over fishing string with
magnets. And she used fibreoptic lighting, which produces very
little heat and therefore could be placed close to the textiles, to
enhance details and create a dramatic shadow.

In a recent lecture at the Architectural League of New York,
Toshiko Mori said it is not simply the material but how it is used
that makes the difference. She illustrated the point by showing
how differently Mies, Kahn and Wright used brick. 'New
production processes are open,' she said, 'function may follow
the form.' She described Homosote that is perforated to admit
light and embedded with resin for strength. She talked about
making plywood from fast-growth trees, aerating materials to
lighten them and making new materials by lamination, the way
the latest America's Cup sailing boats are made.

At Harvard, Mori invited Shiguru Ban to talk about
his paper tube arch over the MoMA garden. She has
been working with the people at the Cal Tech jet-
propulsion laboratory and collaborating with Michael
Sima of the Massachusetts Institute of Technology (MIT),
and Jacques Herzog as well as James Carpenter.

She has also raised $100,000 for a student competition
to create a fence around the construction site for Pei Cobb
Freed's new social science building next door to the
Graduate School of Design. One team will work with
woven plywood, the other with photo luminescence which
will add light and colour to the impersonal barrier on the
street. One of her Harvard studios is structured around
materials that Sheila Kennedy, Merrill Elam and Laurie
Hawkinson (all of whom practise with their domestic
partners) use in work done in their offices. Materials
research, it seems, like charity, begins at home. ⌂

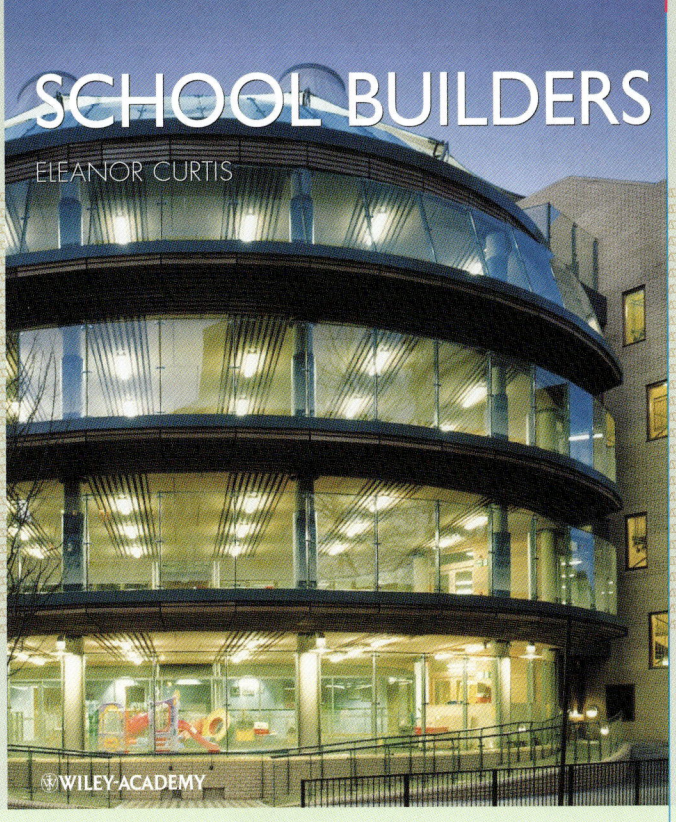

SCHOOL BUILDERS Eleanor Curtis

Educational policies and trends are continually changing, and consequently design briefs for school buildings are also in a constant state of flux. Whether these changes are curriculum driven or socially directed is not as important as the way the school builder equips his or her own architecture to deal with these changes.

School Builders, the latest publication in the successful 'Builders' series by Wiley-Academy, introduces 29 projects from across the globe that are each testimony to these many changes affecting school buildings. Through these projects, which are presented by way of descriptive texts, plans and extensive colour photography, the book introduces a number of pressing and sensitive issues relevant to both the architect and the school governor, and argues the case for flexibility in design.

The examples of school buildings from Europe, the US and Asia cover a wide range of types of brief: from the technology-led classroom to the sustainable 'green' school; from the tight urban vertical site to wide expansive fields; from 100-plus students to almost 4500 students; from the involvement of children and the community; from state to private; and from safety and security to freedom and horizons.

Within this range of issues, *School Builders* shows new technologies to be the main driving force behind the most rapid changes in school design. Technology has allowed schools and learning to change, both in the sense of the physical space as well as in the type of activity happening in that space. Learning can now take place in many different spaces, using many different tools, and at different times for groups or for individuals. In addition, the hardware and software of the tools are themselves constantly changing, making their own demands on the space.

As a way to manage these changes, school buildings must offer more and more flexibility in their design. They need to be able to accommodate potential changes concerning technology, demographics, green and sustainable policies, urban regeneration, safety and security, and all within (mostly) public budgets. And on top of this, do so using creative design solutions. Looking at projects by architects such as Itsuko Hasegawa, American firm Perkins & Will, English firm Hampshire County Council Architects, German firm plus+ bauplanung led by Peter Hübner, the London office of Ove Arup working in India, German firm Behnisch & Partners, and many more, the challenging issue of flexibility in school design is examined in depth. ∆

School Builders (hardback, 224 pages, £50, ISBN 0471623776) is available from John Wiley & Sons Ltd, 1 Oldlands Way, Bognor Regis, West Sussex PO22 9SA, UK. Tel: 0800 243407 (UK freephone) or +44 (0)1243 843303 (from overseas). Fax: +44 (0)1243 843303. Email: cs-books@wiley.co.uk.

Stephen Gage describes how he and Phil Ayres of 16*makers embarked on designing a tree house for his daughter Isobel.

An examination of the more upmarket broadsheets in the UK shows that the ancient profession of arboreal architect is alive and well, and that some substantial (and substantially expensive) tree houses have in fact been commissioned recently.

There are plausible reasons for this, which include a general rise in private expenditure on gardens and landscaping, the loss of the street and the park as places for unstructured play and the demographic shift to late parenthood with consequential parental inertia and a declining enthusiasm for manual skills.

Most tree-house builders take their inspiration either directly or indirectly from the 18th century and specifically from Jean Jacques Rousseau. They construct rustic or sophisticated primitive huts in trees. The tree hut can be noble in a grand tree in a large garden, but it gets progressively more absurd the more urban the garden and the smaller the tree that is in it.

I began to discuss with Phil Ayres, my teaching partner at the Bartlett School of Architecture, the design of Isobel Gage's tree house in 2001, looking for a more elegant and more appropriate solution.

A sophisticated tree house was first described by GK Chesterton in his book *A Club of Queer Trades* published in 1905. It is described as being 'an enormous, dark egg-shaped thing, pendant in the branches like a wasp's nest' and 'hanging by a cunning mechanism' which caused it to 'swing only slightly' in a full gale. This tree house is clearly a grand affair, requiring two large trees for the support, but certain aspects are of considerable interest to the urban arboreal architect – specifically this is not a house in a tree but is more like a nest that is interactive and responsive to its location.

Our early decision was to create a place that would respond to its location, changing shape as branches moved in the wind which would respond to its occupants by deforming as they played in it. A large object in a small tree can look very large, and can also shade an already shady garden to a point where grass and plants find it difficult to grow. Consequently it was decided to make the enclosure translucent, to allow light transmission but also to catch and hold the moving shadows of the tree, the client and her friends. The initial idea was to

construct a large translucent bud in the tree that would keep the weather out; but this was vetoed because it would keep spiders in. The final concept is halfway between a flower and a boat, where two petals of translucent polycarbonate are wrapped around a plywood base. The fluid geometry of the petals evolved through a series of model experiments by Phil Ayres.

Solid polycarbonate sheet is very strong and flexible. It was banned for a time in central London because it presented a safety risk to vandals; it would bounce bricks back with the velocity with which they were thrown (this account dates from 1972 and is absolutely true). It is an excellent and underused architectural resource. A translucent base was also considered – but was thought to be incompatible with the budget. The base, access trap and access ladder were constructed out of two 25-millimetre plywood sheets.

It was agreed that, as far as possible, only plywood and polycarbonate sheet would be used in the proposal. Special wedge fixings were designed by Phil Ayres and were also fabricated in polycarbonate sheet. These are the most highly stressed components in the design and two failed after a particularly energetic tree house party; they are currently being replaced with zinc-sprayed steel.

The tree house was fabricated in the Bartlett workshop and was erected by Phil, to the client's increasing elation, over a day in late spring 2002. It has proved to be a great success. ⊅

Stephen Gage is Professor of Innovative Technology at the Bartlett. He teaches at the Bartlett with Phil Ayres of 16*makers. Gage and Ayres are both members of The Bartlett Interactive Architecture Workshop, projects of which have been reported in ⊅ *Architecture in Cyberspace II* and ⊅ *Reflexive Architecture*.

Subscribe Now for 2003

As an influential and prestigious architectural publication, *Architectural Design* has an almost unrivalled reputation worldwide. Published bimonthly, it successfully combines the currency and topicality of a newsstand journal with the editorial rigour and design qualities of a book. Consistently at the forefront of cultural thought and design since the 1960s, it has time and again proved provocative and inspirational – inspiring theoretical, creative and technological advances. Prominent in the 1980s for the part it played in Postmodernism and then in Deconstruction, △ has recently taken a pioneering role in the technological revolution of the 1990s. With groundbreaking titles dealing with cyberspace and hypersurface architecture, it has pursued the conceptual and critical implications of high-end computer software and virtual realities △

△ Architectural Design

SUBSCRIPTION RATES 2003
Institutional Rate: UK £160
Personal Rate: UK £99
Discount Student* Rate: UK £70
OUTSIDE UK
Institutional Rate: US $240
Personal Rate: US $150
Student* Rate: US $105

*Proof of studentship will be required when placing an order. Prices reflect rates for a 2002 subscription and are subject to change without notice.

TO SUBSCRIBE
Phone your credit card order:
+44 (0)1243 843 828

Fax your credit card order to:
+44 (0)1243 770 432

Email your credit card order to:
cs-journals@wiley.co.uk

Post your credit card or cheque order to:
John Wiley & Sons Ltd.
Journals Administration Department
1 Oldlands Way
Bognor Regis
West Sussex PO22 9SA
UK

Please include your postal delivery address with your order.

All △ volumes are available individually. To place an order please write to:
John Wiley & Sons Ltd
Customer Services
1 Oldlands Way
Bognor Regis
West Sussex PO22 9SA

Please quote the ISBN number of the issue(s) you are ordering.

△ is available to purchase on both a subscription basis and as individual volumes

○ I wish to subscribe to △ *Architectural Design* at the **Institutional rate of £160**.

○ I wish to subscribe to △ *Architectural Design* at the **Personal rate of £99**.

○ I wish to subscribe to △ *Architectural Design* at the **Student rate of £70**.

STARTING FROM ISSUE 1/2003.

○ Payment enclosed by Cheque/Money order/Drafts.

Value/Currency £/US$ [_____]

○ Please charge £/US$ [_____] to my credit card.
Account number:

[ ][ ][ ][ ][ ][ ][ ][ ][ ][ ][ ][ ][ ][ ][ ][ ]

Expiry date:

[ ][ ][ ][ ][ ]

Card: Visa/Amex/Mastercard/Eurocard *(delete as applicable)*

Cardholder's signature [_____]

Cardholder's name [_____]

Address [_____]

[_____]

[_____] Post/Zip Code [_____]

Recipient's name [_____]

Address [_____]

[_____]

[_____] Post/Zip Code [_____]

I would like to buy the following Back Issues at £22.50 each:

○ △ 160 *Food + Architecture*, Karen A Franck

○ △ 159 *Versioning in Architecture*, SHoP

○ △ 158 *Furniture + Architecture*, Edwin Heathcote

○ △ 157 *Reflexive Architecture*, Neil Spiller

○ △ 156 *Poetics in Architecture*, Leon van Schaik

○ △ 155 *Contemporary Techniques in Architecture*, Ali Rahim

○ △ 154 *Fame and Architecture*, J. Chance and T. Schmiedeknecht

○ △ 153 *Looking Back in Envy*, Jan Kaplicky

○ △ 152 *Green Architecture*, Brian Edwards

○ △ 151 *New Babylonians*, Iain Borden + Sandy McCreery

○ △ 150 *Architecture + Animation*, Bob Fear

○ △ 149 *Young Blood*, Neil Spiller

○ △ 148 *Fashion and Architecture*, Martin Pawley

○ △ 147 *The Tragic in Architecture*, Richard Patterson

○ △ 146 *The Transformable House*, Jonathan Bell and Sally Godwin

○ △ 145 *Contemporary Processes in Architecture*, Ali Rahim

○ △ 144 *Space Architecture*, Dr Rachel Armstrong

○ △ 143 *Architecture and Film II*, Bob Fear

○ △ 142 *Millennium Architecture*, Maggie Toy and Charles Jencks

○ △ 141 *Hypersurface Architecture II*, Stephen Perrella

○ △ 140 *Architecture of the Borderlands*, Teddy Cruz

○ △ 139 *Minimal Architecture II*, Maggie Toy

○ △ 138 *Sci-Fi Architecture*, Maggie Toy

○ △ 137 *Des-Res Architecture*, Maggie Toy